HOW TO ANALYZE PEOPLE

CARL DOLTON

Copyright © 2020 by Carl Dolton

All rights reserved. No part of this book may be used or reproduced by any means, graphic, electronic, or mechanical, including photocopying, recording, taping, or by any information storage retrieval system, without the written permission of the publisher except in the case of brief quotations embodied in critical articles and reviews.

Table of Contents

Introduction 1

Chapter 1: Where Do We Begin With Analysis?....4

What's Going On In Our Brains? 4

The Subconscious... 4

The Science Of Human Behavior........................... 7

Chapter 2: First Impressions 10

What Are We Looking For? 10

Create Your Own Baseline For Guidance 15

Chapter 3: Nature V Nuture 23

Nature 23

Nurture 26

Chapter 4: Key Personality Traits 37

Personality And Character Traits........................... 37

Why We Should Not Be Too Quick To Judge 46

Chapter 5: Body Language 49

Reading Body Language For Personality Clues...... 49

Facial Expressions.. 50

Hands And Arms... 55

Feet And Legs 59
Body Posture 63
Appearance 71

Chapter 6: Dark Psychology 76
The Dark Triad 78
Traits Of The Dark Triad Personality 81
How Do You Escape A Controlling Relationship? . 88

Chapter 7: Cultures And Beliefs 106
Religion And Behavior 106
Social Media And Desensitization 109
Education 112

Chapter 8: Can People Change Their Personality? 115
Clinical Intervention 116
How Do You Change Your Personality? 119
How To Control Anxiety 131
Discontentment Of The Self 135

Conclusion 140

Introduction

As a teenager, I often got into the habit of watching people and assessing them. It fired up my curiosity as I began to realize how unique every single person on this planet is. We all have some attributes in common, such as inherited genes. But, we also develop individual traits that can stay with us for life.

I hadn't chosen my career path at that point, though I knew I wanted to be successful wherever it would lead me. With my interest in analyzing people, I felt I would enjoy leadership or politics. Or even any kind of negotiation job, such as sales, business, or diplomacy. This took my curiosity to another level and I chose to study psychology. It was the right choice because it taught me how to read other people's character traits honestly and fairly. If you want to analyze people, you cannot afford to be judgmental of their behavior and beliefs.

In my book, I want to share with you how you too can learn to analyze people in an open and non-judgmental way. Learn why it's vital to comprehend what's going on in their minds. The subconscious can give away secrets in your behavior well before you even realize what's happening. Teach yourselves to avoid this.

To begin the process of analyzing people, you need to understand specific personality patterns. This can help choose certain people for specific tasks. It's good to know who might be good under pressure. That way you can pick someone who will remain calm and help those around them stay calm too, during a stressful situation.

We spend much of our lives learning how to get on with other people. By being more connected with the people around us, it can lead to better respect and popularity. This increases our chances of being more successful, and not only in our choice of careers. Being a better person because we can empathize. That's because we've taken the time to know how important this trait can be.

Though, before you can get inside the minds of other people, you need to first understand yourself. What's going on in your own head? Are there any personality traits you need to look at changing, that will help you become that better person? You can't find solutions to a problem unless you know where the obstacles lay. By developing a working pattern of baseline behavior, you will find solutions to help yourself and others to become more positive.

You also need to learn how to evade negative misunderstandings. It's good to expand on the main 5 behavioral traits known as OCEAN, to better yourself. But you will also need to be aware of the darker personality traits, that can hold you back. People who are ruled by the darker traits can be very demanding and even quite cruel. Learn how to spot them, or even how to avoid them.

This book doesn't only focus on teaching you how to analyze other people, but also how to analyze yourself. Discover things you most likely didn't know about yourself. Only then can you celebrate your distinctive strengths and help others to help themselves.

Chapter 1

Where Do We Begin with Analysis?

What's going on in our brains?

As sentient beings, we analyze our surroundings every day of our lives

Some of us do it at work, such as comparing statistics to put them in an order to provide useful information to help make decisions. Or, a student will research information to analyze a particular topic and pass exams.

Our brains are so busy analyzing life all around us, every second of every day. We sift through vast levels of information and the action is so integrated into our daily lives, that we're not even aware we're doing it.

The Subconscious

A common analogy of the human brain is the similarities to a powerful computer. We fill and organize databases with information on computers. Much the same mechanism exists in a brain. As we experience life, we store away memories that we can often recall to help us make decisions in life.

The truth is that scientists don't yet understand how the brain works. Though they do know that the two states of consciousness and subconscious exist. It's believed that the human brain can process up to 400 billion bits in any one second. Yet, the conscious parts of the brain can only process around 2000 of those bits. That's a huge difference between the two states, so what's going on?

It's when we fall asleep that our subconscious mind seems to take control. All those memories and information held in there, come to the forefront of our minds. As we still don't have full control of the subconscious, the information tends to get a little muddled. This confusion plays out in our dreams.

Often, the information that we're busy storing when we're awake, doesn't even register in our conscious. We are not even aware that we're storing it. For instance, when you're shopping in a store, your eyes will focus on the products that you're interested in. You're thinking about those products as you look for them, using your conscious state. At the same time, your brain's busy storing information on other products in your periphery view. Have you ever forgotten something in the store and then thought to yourself, "Oh yes, I passed that a few isles down." How do you know that, when you weren't even focusing on it? Yet, your subconscious noticed it and is now making you aware of it.

People who meditate can learn to reach deeper into the subconscious parts of the mind. It's believed to help restore emotional balance. If we can tap into all that information, then is it possible to change how we think and behave?

The subconscious is a very powerful tool. It's a good resource when it comes to analyzing everyday life. Human behavior is often led by what's in the subconscious. We often do things without thinking and some believe this shows a person's true character. By observing human behavior, it will help you analyze a person's character, but it is the true one?

Observing behavior alone is not enough to help you analyze a person's personality. You also need an understanding of what processes are affecting their subconsciousness. With a good balance of information, only then can you analyze why people behave in certain ways. Learning the basics of psychology is necessary when it comes to analyzing people. It's also useful if you wish to learn how to control your own behavior. Then you can govern how other's might perceive you.

The Science of Human Behavior

Scientists have shown that the brain controls our emotions, behavior, and everything about us. It's an amazing organ, driven by chemical reactions and electrical signals. As it's responsible for the negative and positive feelings we experience, it's worth understanding how it functions. Does it mean that we're all the same?

Let's take siblings as an example. They have a very similar upbringing, but does that mean that they will behave in exactly the same way? Although they share similar experiences, one may be shy and another more confident. One may be quiet and reserved and another loud and boisterous. How can this be if they've had similar experiences in their lives?

This is where the sciences came into practice. Sigmond Freud is one of the original psychologists from the nineteenth century. He devised a standard mechanism of the mind. Freud's studies show that the human mind is driven by three typical sets of behavior, the Id, Ego, and Superego. The id represents our subconscious. This, he believed, is the main driver of human behavior. The ego drives us to seek things that please us. Whereas the superego is more about how social influences around us can control us. If we can learn to cast aside our egotistic nature, the ego, supposedly we will become better people.

One study in 2016, at a Madrid university, showed there are in fact four main behavioral types. It indicated that 90% of the population is either optimistic, pessimistic, trusting, or envious. Of those, 30% were envious, and the other sections equaled 20% each. The remaining 10% of the population could not be determined in any of the outlined groups. Does this mean that the 30% who were envious, were neither optimistic nor pessimistic?

There are many studies around the world, all showing the complexities of human behavior. To use such statements in your analysis, you should scrutinize the data that led to their results. That way, you can be confident that your own analytical processes are correct.

There are many theories of psychology and human behavior, and you don't need to learn them all. You don't even need to use any particular one for your analysis. As every human has individual behavior patterns, it shows the complexities of this subject. If you wish to analyze human behavior, then it's worth learning the fundamental aspects of what drives us to make decisions. Only then can you surmise why one person is more optimistic than another, or more confident than shy. Analysis should reflect true facts.

Chapter 2

FIRST IMPRESSIONS

What are we looking for?

Most of us, don't usually go about our lives never talking to strangers. The chances are that you will smile at a stranger, and even converse with politeness. After all, it doesn't matter what impression they have of you because you're not likely to ever see them again.

That's all normal and civilized behavior but what happens when a stranger is about to become a part of your life? Are you going to be more judgmental in how you view that person?

The Primacy Effect is a science-based approach that shows how we tend to remember the first and last parts of something we're assessing. The middle part is all but forgotten. For instance, if you have a list of words to remember, this is likely what will happen. When it comes to meeting people, it's a little different but nonetheless, we are very much influenced by what's at the beginning.

First impressions are influenced by as much as 55%, on what we see before us.

Here are a few eye opening studies that indicate this to be true.

Study 1 Dress Sense

How a person dresses can determine whether you believe them to be respectable or not. A Dutch study in 2011, showed that those wearing expensive clothing are seen as higher status figures. Whilst those not wearing branded clothing are seen as further down the ladder of respectability.

In 2013, a Turkish study showed that men dressed in tailored suits were seen as more successful than men dressed in ill-fitting suits.

A Canadian study, in 2011, indicated that well-dressed men were seen as more successful. They were also more likely to be chosen for promotion.

Study 2 Trusting

A Princeton study reveals that first are determined in 1/10th of a second. A. Todorov's research showed that the first thing we observe is whether or not the stranger before us is attractive or not. This is regardless of gender. If they're not deemed as attractive, we can then be guilty of dismissing them in an instant.

Study 3 Racial Bias

A Toronto University study, in 2017, reveals how much racial bias can affect first impressions. In this experiment, students watched a recording of a speech with no sound. They were asked to rate charisma and leadership. By body language alone, the results were astounding. It suggested that those seen as attractive did better. People who used more eye contact and didn't wear glasses were also rated higher. Even more contentious is how racial heritage affected the results. Those of Caucasian origin were favored higher.

Study 4 Voice Tone

The tone of voice also plays an influencing role. A Miami university experiment made clear in their 2012 study. Students listened to voice recordings, with no other stimulus. The voice was saying, "Vote for me." Both men and women with a low pitch to their tone came out on top. For the female candidates, the students believed that the low pitch meant they were more trustworthy. For men, the lower pitch made them sound stronger.

Study 5 Stereotypes

When it comes to stereotypes, a British study in 2007 highlighted some surprising results. Women with tattoos were labeled as promiscuous, heavy drinkers.

On the same theme, s Polish study found that tattooed men were seen by other men as more masculine and dominant. Whilst women viewed those same men as untrustworthy partners.

On this note, a study by Pennsylvania University indicated an odd result. Bald men were seen as more dominant than men with a full head of hair.

Research shows the popular traits that we're looking for in our first impressions. We're assessing if a person is happy or sad, boisterous or reserved, confident or nervous, all in a few milliseconds. Their posture will a sign of how confident they are. This will include how much eye contact they have with you, or if they fold their arms as a barrier. Yet, there may be other reasons for folded arms - they could be cold. See how easy we can get our assessment wrong!

What we're doing is labeling other people's looks and actions. Then again, it takes time to get to know the personality dwelling within that outer shell. How then can we stop ourselves going by that first impression?

Throughout our lives, we develop a belief in stereotypical views of people. It's those neurological processes kicking in again. Our subconscious is busy influencing our thoughts without us even realizing it. Oh, and let's not forget how influenced we are by other people's opinions. And, that's even before you set eyes on them.

Even if you're not so quick off the mark in your judgment, there will be other outside influences directing your views. Your mood on the day and the environment you're in. will all be affecting your assessment. It's easy to see why we shouldn't allow first impressions to be the only impression we have of someone.

It's important not to take too much at face value. If you think about it, these are all very judgmental views when you haven't even spoken to the person yet. It shows how easily influenced we can be by first impressions. In those first few seconds, you've most likely judged whether the person before you is attractive or ugly, and friend or foe.

Science tells us though, that our initial assessment is actually based on self-preservation.

You can't scientifically measure what your eyes are seeing, so be careful, you may get it wrong!

Wouldn't it be better to have full control over all that analysis going on in your head?

Create your own baseline for guidance

To help you anayze other people, create your own baseline of expectations. That way you're not going to be over influenced by that first impression.

Should we take into account other people's opinions of someone?

Would you want strangers to assess you on someone else's opinion?

It's unlikely. We all want a chance to prove ourselves before being judged.

Unless it's an official situation such as a job interview, then don't allow second-hand opinions to cloud your judgement. Those opinions may be biased and therefore clouding of the truth.

If someone tells you that a certain person isn't honest, ask for the facts first. Better still, use a baseline, that we'll show you how to create, to help you make fairer judgments. Keep an open mind until you have done your guided analysis.

YOU get to decide which traits you believe are important.

It will be a baseline not only for first meetings, but to enable you to assess a person as you get to know them. That means not being judgmental right from the word 'go'.

An example of a baseline could be:

How often do they smile? Let's face it, no one wants unfriendly people in their lives.

Are they talking too loud and if so, why? It could be that they're a little deaf, or nervous. Or it could be that they're controlling and make sure that they are heard by all. This is a trait that needs analyzing deeper.

Do they appear to be honest? Learn to tell when people are lying to you, which we'll cover later in the book.

To some extent, we already create ourselves a baseline, but it will not have structure. How we already perceive people, unless we've given it this kind of thought, will be based on our instincts, which can often be wrong. That's why it's better if you are the one to set the conscious guidelines. Do this and you won't be allowing your subconscious to make all the decisions for you. It also allows you to analyze everyone in the same way, no matter what mood you're in on the day. It should be a fairer system that's not influenced by emotions.

Let's look at an example of how a baseline might help:

A mother has an argument with her teenage son before setting off to work.

It puts her in a bad mood.

At work, she's interviewing applicants for a Saturday job in the store where she works.

The first candidate is a teenage male and without thinking, her reaction is, "no way, he's not having the job." This decision is likely because of her previous altercation with her own teenager.

It is an unfair and wrong judgment but we don't see it that way unless we have a baseline to go by.

She has allowed her subconscious thoughts to take over her assessment.

On top of that, she's has used a stereotypical view of how ALL teenagers behave.

She needs to put aside her unconscious thoughts and use her baseline guide. That way she will avoid being judgemental without thought.

Now let's look at her possible baseline guide:

She has created herself a system for determining how to judge people. It reminds her to look for the potential of a person and not go by the initial meeting or stereotypical views. She smiles at herself as she remembers using this system when she met her daughter's new boyfriend for the first time. In fact, she uses this system whenever she meets new people.

The specific traits she's looking for are –

FRIENDLINESS

How often does this person smile?

Someone who smiles too much might be nervous or they may be faking it.

Therefore -

Is their smile in the right context?

If they smile out of context in a conversation, it could be a sign that they're not paying attention.

Does their smile extend to their eyes?

When we smile, it's not only with our lips. We use around twelve different muscles in the face. One of the key muscles is the Orbicularis oculi and it creates laugh lines around the eyes. if it's an open mouth smile and the bottom teeth are showing, the chances are it's a fake smile. No one opens their mouth that wide unless they're laughing out loud.

If their smile looks false then it needs further investigation.

How much eye contact does this person use?

If a person cannot manage good eye contact in conversation it could mean that they're either nervous or shy. Or, it could mean that they're not paying attention.

We're more likely to remember a person if they have good, relaxed eye contact with us.

It's more important to use eye contact if you are listening than if you are the one doing the talking. It shows you are focused on the other person.

Is this person dressed appropriately for the situation?

We all know the difference between a casual outfit and a smart one. This makes it easy to judge if the other person is making an effort or not. What we wear depends on the situation we're in. Other people will be observing without even thinking about what they're seeing. If you're dressed inappropriately, they will be judging you, so make the effort, it's worth it.

What does this person do with their hands and arms ie are they fidgeting, or are they using them as barriers? OR, *How does this person sit, or stand ie are they relaxed or stiff?*

Open gestures indicate that a person is relaxed.

See our chapter on body language so you can learn what to look out for.

The list of what should be on your basic assessment sheet will be quite long. The idea is to judge everyone with the same set of questions in your head. The good traits that pass your analysis will help to see the positives. However, look deeper into the actions that are noted by your observations. There may be a simple explanation for any negative behavior, but at least you have alerted yourself to it. For instance, if someone keeps covering their mouth with their hands, you might consider them nervous. Then again, they may be covering their mouth because they have a facial spot that they're conscious of. That's a negative trait turned into a positive one, so be careful before you make your final assessment.

At first, you may need to write your list down. Create it when you can consciously think about it. *What qualities do want to look for that you like? How will you investigate negative qualities further?* It might seem complex to start with but if you make a physical list, it should start to make sense. In time, you'll have asked yourself the same questions many times over, and you'll soon know them without the need for a written list. What you have achieved, though, is the ability to analyze another person by using your conscious. You have put thought into what you perceive as good qualities and taught yourself to look for them. You've also taught yourself to investigate any bad qualities, without being too judgmental in the beginning.

Let's now have a look at the many factors to take into consideration to help you create that baseline guide.

Chapter 3

NATURE V NUTURE

Nature

Nature refers to the stuff that's prewired in our minds and body. This incorporates things like genes and hormones, it's our genetic makeup.

Nurture is more about external events, such as our surroundings and the people around us.

Without a doubt, the people around us will influence our outlook on life. But, genetics plays a very important role in determining personality too. There have been a few studies of twins who live separate lives, yet still having similar personalities. It's because, monozygotic, or identical twins, have both inherited the same DNA. It also happens with adopted children. Their personality will still be influenced by their biological parents, even though they don't live with them or even know who they are. Research shows that we are influenced by our caregivers at a very young age. As we develop, then our genes are more likely to direct our personality traits, (Harris 2006 and Roberts & DelVecchio, 2000).

Without getting into too much technical detail, we can still take a look at the fundamentals of nurture vs nature.

Genes

Let's start with our inherited genes.

Chromosomes are in the segmented parts of our DNA (deoxyribonucleic acid), *known as genes.*

Within each cell of our body, there are around 46 chromosomes. They're divided up into 23 pairs, each with one chromosome from each of our biological parents. What's surprising is that 99.9% of human genes are identical. It's the same for all species. This is what drives each species to behave in similar ways (Tinbergen 1951). For example, birds build nests, monkeys climb trees, and humans strive for innovation.

The identical genes play a big part in collective behavior. A National Institute of Health research shows that there are around 25,000 human genes. What helps to make us different is that we all inherit different combinations of these thousands of genes. Yet, in humans, only 0.1% of our genes will be different from someone else's. But this is enough to make us individual to one another.

Your genetic material determines how you look. Certain chromosomes will be the deciding factor on whether you will be tall or short. They will determine the color of hair and eyes. So, there will many brown-eyed, tall people out there but they won't have the same personality. Though, scientific studies also tell us that 20-60% of our inherited genes will determine our behavior too. Even things such as whether we're early risers or night birds. That's because genes are part of the link between the brain and the cells where our genes are.

Here are a few examples of some genes and their names:

MAOA (monoamine oxidase A). Linked to introversion.

DRD2 and 4 (Domanine). Linked to a need to seek adventure.

CFTR (cystic fibrosis transmembrane conductance regulator). A protein-making gene linked to cystic fibrosis.

Hormones

Hormones are the chemicals your body produces. They are released from glands and they affect your emotions and behavior. For instance, if something frightens you, the shock floods your system with adrenaline, a chemical. Your brain has informed your body to prepare you for the fight or flight reaction. The heart will beat faster and you'll breath quicker too, all because of the chemical reaction in your body.

It's not surprising that these chemicals affect your moods. Emotions are also linked to our behavior and personality.

It's easy to see now how the combination of genes and hormones work together to make your personality.

There is one more important element to add to this recipe. It involves what is going on around you. This will include the environment you live in. Plus, the people who influence your decisions in life. This is known as nurture.

Nurture

Your environment and the people who raise you will, to some extent, help to create your personality.

Whether you're brought up with wealth or in poverty will also be influencing factors. The friends or enemies that you make will also play their part in molding your character. All the while, those genes, and hormones inside your body are directing your emotions and reactions to the outside world.

Given the link between cells and the brain, it helps to understand the science of psychology. It too plays a part in helping us to understand who we are, and why we behave as we do.

Psychology

Psychologists have developed many theories about personality development. Different things affect us in various stages of our lives. Two such eminent psychologists are Freud and Erikson.

Freud covers the early stages in life with his psychosexual stages.

1 Oral Stage – n the first year of life, our experiences are focused through the mouth. This is when a bond develops with the mother. Those whose needs are not met may develop mistrust and outbursts of anger. The need to shout out their frustrations.

2 Anal Stage – At this stage, we develop an understanding of shame and doubting ourselves. Given encouragement and not punishment, the child will become confident.

3 Genital Stage – We're becoming more aware of ourselves and the different sexes. We're also competing with siblings more. We're noticing that what we want isn't necessarily what our parents/carers want. Conflicts begin and this is a stage where we can learn that lying is easy.

Erikson covers the later stages with his Psychosocial development.

4 Latency Stage – We're learning to be industrious as we begin our schooling. We may become confident and responsible. Or, we may develop feelings of inferiority that cause us to withdraw and become more introvert.

5 Adolescence Stage – We want to be treated as equals, if it doesn't happen then we may rebel. Without realizing, we often look for role models. Let's hope we chose the right one because we're very influenced by our peers

Each stage plays an important role in who we are, and what kind of adults we'll make. This leads on to what sort of character we develop, according to which personality traits we gain.

The Changing Characters of Ageing

You might believe that you're still the same person in your middle years as you were in your youth. Studies show that there is a degree of personality plasticity (changes) as we age. It's true that we do tend to become 'wiser'. Even more confident, but only because we become more relaxed in our views. Although some inherited traits don't change. It's unlikely that you'll become an extrovert if you're a natural introvert.

Let's have a look at what many of these studies consider is 'typical' behavior of people by their age.

Early Years

It's easy to see how our personality can be influenced by nurture in our early years. We're very dependent on the people who care for us. This means that they are the people who will have the biggest influence on our development. We'll rely on them to teach us how to behave. They tell us what is right and wrong, in their view. Their wealth, or lack of it, will also drive out outlook on life.

Teenage Years

Once the teenage years begin, many of us turn into monsters overnight. Well, not quite, but we do tend to rebel at this age, no matter what kind of background we've had. We're now finding our individuality. We want to become more independent from those around us, particularly the adults. It's now that our caregivers have less influence over us, and instead, we turn to our peers. Our environment and friend groups will either become larger or smaller, depending on how confident we've grown.

Lots of growing is happening within the brain in our teenage years, as neurons develop like twigs on a tree. The hippocampus (memory) in the brain will be growing as these are our years of education. Is this the mystery as to why teenagers are always so tired because the brain is so busy?

These are the years our attitude to life tends to start forming. Attitude is an important part of your personality so let's have a look at how it can be perceived by others.

What is Attitude?

A person's attitude is a result of what they have learned through their experiences in life. In some respects, it is a label of how others perceive your behavior. Without knowing you well, others will have an opinion of your attitude, or approach, to life.

Those perceived to have a good attitude often have a more positive outlook on life. This is a person who maintains a positive mindset, no matter what experiences they encounter. They seek out the 'good' in every situation, and in people too. Such a person will be confident and learn by their mistakes rather than dwelling on them.

People with a poorer attitude are often considered to have tunnel vision. They will be saddled with doubts, frustrations, and most likely anger. They may be quite opinionated and not open to other people's views. It could be that their upbringing did not allow for freedom of thought, so as adults they don't know how to open up.

It's worth mentioning here that there is a difference between character and personality traits. We know that many of the basic personality traits lean more towards inherited genes. Our attitude though, is more to do with our character, and our character is molded from our experiences. Attitude is a learned trait. It stems from the things going on around you as you grow-up, all of will influence you to develop some kind of attitude.

Twenties

Once through the tribulations of our teenage years, most of us start to leave the wild experimentations of self-discovery behind. By now, we're less reliant on adults telling us how to behave. Instead, we continue our attempt to understand the world around us and start to make mature decisions ourselves. Some may decide they want to make the world a better place. Others may only be concerned with themselves. Some are driven to be successful in their occupation, others have little motivation to be under the thumb of yet more bossy adults. Many even become parents as they begin to fit into the role of adulthood.

Thirties

In the 1890s, Harvard Psychologist, W James, stated that a person's personality is set like plaster by the time they reach their thirties. This belief is still popular today. By our thirties, our lives tend to be in some form of routine. We also tend to be more emotionally stable. Gone are the days of being anxious over what you wear and how you look. By the time you reach your 30s, you're more comfortable with yourself and less caring about what other people think. That doesn't mean to say you don't like to be fashionable, but you're not driven by peer pressure so much. Although you will have gained core beliefs that are more fixed and unmovable.

This is only a generalization and not set in stone. It's worth noting that when you're analyzing someone past their twenties, they may be easier to read because of their acceptance of stability.

Forties

This is an age when there will be lots of hormonal changes taking place in the aging body. Particularly for women, who can enter the menopause at any time from their forties onwards. Even the timing of menopause is determined by inherited genes. If your mother entered the menopause early, the likelihood is that you will too. As hormones affect mood changes, these are the years when women's behavior can be dictated by their hormonal changes.

The forties are also the years when regrets begin to arise and we tend to wish we'd done more with our lives. Often referred to as the midlife crisis. Some may welcome a change in their career, so they can achieve a goal of doing something new before they 'get too old'. Others are more set in their ways and unwilling to try new things so late on in life.

People in their forties tend to be less self-critical than what they were in their earlier lives. This is an age when our confidence starts to stabilize and we become more accepting of what's going on around us.

Fifties

Our fifties will bring about changes that can be related to health. Our bodies are aging, especially if we haven't lived a particularly healthy lifestyle. Arguably, this is nothing to do with our personality. Yet, such factors will affect our behavior because all these processes are interlinked. As we age, our personality becomes more settled and we become more the person who we truly are. That's the person starts to accept their inherited traits and knows they can't change who they are. Along with the person who has experienced life and finally begins to accept all that's been thrown at them. At this stage in our lives, we are likely more trustworthy and more open.

Sixties

Sixties is the time when retirement looms for many. Chances you and you've seen and experienced much going on in your world. Governments have come and gone and you accept that their promises are empty. In general, you expect less from society. By these years, you're not so judgmental. Instead, you have more patience for those around you, and you're more forgiving of other people's mistakes. If we all had this kind of attitude in our twenties, the world would be a more peaceful place.

Old Age

Hopefully, by your seventies, eighties, or even nineties, you deserve to rest and take life at a slower pace. There's no need to be a part of the 'rat race' anymore. Sit back and observe others having a go at what your own generation failed at. It's a circle that we will all do.

Summary

Don't be guilty of allowing first impressions to cloud your judgment. It's worth learning some of the different personality traits that deeply influence a person's attitude to life. And then understanding how's those traits can change over our lifespan. What we're showing here is that age plays a big role in personality changes.

To analyze other people, delve deeper into how they have developed their maturing personality. Younger people are harder to read because they have more complex personalities. Are we different people in our twenties to what they are in retirement age? Well, research indicates that we are, and for the better.

Chapter 4

KEY PERSONALITY TRAITS

Personality and Character Traits

By traits, we are referring to attributes, such as introvert or extrovert. There are a few key traits, and the others are facets that stem from them. Every trait though is affected by nature and nurture influences.

Do you want to understand why people behave as they do?

Then it's better to have a basic grasp of the different personality and character traits. *How else can you read other people's intentions and make your assessment with confidence?*

One very popular study, in the 1970s, showed that there were 5 main traits. To make them easy to learn, they set them out in the creation of the acronym: OCEAN.

O Openness to experiences. This questions how curious you are, or if you are close-minded.

C Conscientiousness – Includes organizational skills, extravagance, and carelessness.

E Extraversion – Whether you're extrovert or introvert.

A Agreeableness – Whether you're challenging or compassionate.

N Neuroticism – Confidence or nervousness.

To analyze people, learning these traits will help you understand what's going on in their minds, their body, and their lives. It will guide you in what drives people to behave as they do.

O OPPENNESS TO EXPERIENCES

Openness is linked to creativity. That may be in art, or even in the sciences but it's also in life itself. An open person is receptive to new experiences and ideas. The opposite person is more locked in their beliefs and unwilling to change.

Many scientific models have studied and analyzed the main traits. We will focus on one such model that suggests there are a further six facets to Openness.

Active Imagination

This refers to the level of artistic creation. Many artists have high levels of openness. But, an active imagination can be a double-edged sword.

Clinical psychologists, Wolfstein and Trull explain this in their study. They suggest that people with an active imagination can be susceptible to mental health issues. Other studies have also shown issues towards those with an openness to fantasy. This trait correlates with a susceptibility to depression. People who enjoy imaginary fantasy may be hiding from reality. It's suggested that this may be a means of controlling your world. Those who do this cannot face the real world as they feel a lack of control.

It's not possible to undo an active imagination as it's most likely an inherited gene. At the same time, don't over-read these negative suggestions. Everyone needs a bit of escapism. Instead, learn to use your imagination positively. If you believe in your ideas, then take them forward and be prepared to push over the hurdles. Don't hide from truths, learn to confront them by accepting failure, and moving on to try again. After all, you'll have millions of ideas on what to do next.

Aesthetically Sensitive

Such people can also have an active imagination. Those who are susceptible to seeking pleasurable experiences may be more sensitive. They are the type of person to experience intensive emotions. Their aesthetic approach will leave them feeling joy, disappointment, pleasure, or even disgust. These people are often introvert in character. Yet, they also seek intellect and learning, so this is not always a negative trait. As with an active imagination, use it to your advantage. Learn to always look for the positives, even in the things you find negative.

Emotional Awareness

If you have emotional awareness, it refers to your inner awareness. You will find it easy to sort out distorted thoughts by using your inner dialogue to analyze your emotions. It gives you an understanding of other people's emotions so you can better evaluate other's. This helps you to find a good balance in life for you and those in your life. You will be the kind of person that treats other people's emotions the same way that you treat your own. You're likely to be a good communicator because you can look at things objectively. If you have this trait, you a person who is very self-aware but in a positive way.

Stress Tolerance

Ever wondered why some people can cope with stress better than others? The likelihood is that it relates to those inherited genes. If you're prone to depression, it could be that you've inherited the genes 3P:25-26. They lay within a certain section of chromosomes. If this gene is dominant, then you'll produce less of the chemical serotonin, causing depression. It also means that you're more likely to suffer from anxiety, and all that's attached to such emotions.

Consideration must also be given to how your primary caregivers managed their own stresses. They will have influenced your ability to cope too, as their behavior will have rubbed off on you.

For some, as they develop in age and maturity, their stress levels may mature too. This means that they may cope better as they age.

See our section on 'The Changing Characters of Ageing,' to understand what can happen on as you get older.

Desire to learn

This is related to how inquisitive you are. Another term for it is 'intellectual curiosity'. This is the human desire to learn and be innovative. It happens in industry, and in the sciences too. Are you the type of person who takes things at face value and accepts that's how it's all meant to be? Or, do you question why everything is as it is, and seek answers and better solutions? Many are happy with the life they have and don't welcome changes. Whereas others are never satisfied with their lot. This type of character will constantly strive to change and improve things around them. Which one are you?

C CONSCIENTIOUSNESS

There are many scientific models to explain 'conscientiousness' so it can be difficult to know which research to believe.

For instance, take the NEO PI (Neuroticism, Extraversion, Openness - Personality Inventory), model. It suggests Conscientiousness is broken down into 6 facets. – Self Discipline, Striving for Achievements, Morals, Desire for Oder, Logic, Competence, and Dutifulness. That's a lot to take in.

For ease of understanding, we'll use a model that suggests Conscientiousness can be broken down into only 2 facets.

Orderliness

This facet relates more to how regimented a person you are. Is your desk tidy and clear, or is it a mess of reports, papers, and pens?

Do you prefer a routine to your day, or go about everything haphazardly?

Some believe perfection is a goal worth achieving but is that true?

A perfectionist can be very annoying for those around them. More so for a non-perfectionist. For those who haven't inherited the right genes, then the search for perfection can be frustrating and unachievable. We should all aim to fall somewhere in the middle because no one likes the office slob either.

Industriousness

An industrious personality is driven to succeed at whatever they do. Generally, they will be willing to work hard to be successful. Industrious characters are not always successful in what they do. But, they tend to accept the mistakes they make and move on to try something another goal.

By using only 2 facets, it's easy to see whether a person is conscientious or not.

E EXTRAVERSION

This is an important trait, and most likely an inherited one. Though confidence can be learned, even if you're a shy person. For the sake of observations in your analysis:

An introvert prefers to be alone. May even be shy and not particularly enjoy being the center of attention. That's not to say they can't be successful because they may be industrious too.

An extrovert loves to socialize. They will usually speak their mind and have lots of self-confidence.

It will depend on where you are on the scales of balance as which traits dominate the most. For instance, you may love to be the center of attention but also be shy as a rule.

A AGREEABLENESS

This is a positive personality trait to have and is most likely connected to your genetic makeup.

It's a person who feels empathy and strives to help others, even to the detriment of their own personal situation. Whilst it is possible to learn empathy if it doesn't come naturally it can be difficult to master. It's more of a natural evolutionary trait. An agreeable person will have this characteristic in abundance. They are genuinely good people. Sometimes so good that they can exhaust themselves because they don't know when to stop. They are trusting people and great to have in your corner.

N NEUROTICISM

This is one of those traits whereby it's best to be on the scale of neuroticism somewhere in the middle.

A neurotic person doesn't tend to be a happy one. They lack confidence in themselves and may likely suffer from depression and anxiety. These are the worrying type of characters. Being very self-conscious they tend to set themselves unbelievable targets that are impossible to reach. They can also be very possessive by nature not willing to share anything.

Some level of neuroticism is beneficial for us all. It's the cynical side of our nature that pushes us to question things before we trust them. For some though, it may be so bad that their neuroticism puts them on the level of suffering a personality disorder, such as compulsive disorder.

To some extent, this trait may be in your genes and never triggered. Then along comes some stressful life experience sets it off. Once triggered, it will be difficult to control.

Why we should not be too quick to judge

What sort of character would you choose in a computer game? It's a time when we get to use that imagination of ours and escape the real world. We'd all rather be seen as brave as opposed to being a coward, and that's easy in a make-believe world. Yet, negative personality traits don't necessarily mean a person is bad or weak.

For instance:

THINKERS

Suppose you have a quick-thinking decisive person, and also an indecisive person. Most of us will believe the quick thinker to have a stronger personality. Yet, could it be that the one not making an immediate decision is weighing up all the odds first? Is that not far wiser?

HARD WORKERS

Suppose you have a hard-working person and a person who works at a much slower pace. Will the slower one be labeled as the lazier of the two? Yet, could it be that the 'lazy' one has health conditions affecting their energy or speed?

BULLIES

We all hate a bully. Often, bullies are people who have suffered the same fate themselves. Given the right type of guidance, they may be able to change this negative character trait.

SUMMARY

What a person lacks in one thing, they may have strengths in others. To know the real answers when analyzing people, assess ALL the facts before making your final judgment. Otherwise, you may get a person's personality all. Make sure that your baseline allows for the whys and wherefores of weaknesses, as well as strengths.

Chapter 5

Body Language

Reading Body Language for Personality Clues

Body language is a huge topic of scientific interest. Studies indicate that 55% of human communication is done through the movements of your body. This is called body language, or nonverbal language. It's no wonder that we are so influenced by first impressions, as we observe the person before us. If you're going to judge someone in an instant, at least use the right tools to do so.

When you first meet a stranger, your brain is processing a barrage of information as you observe a person's body language. Considering the huge influence it has on our decision making, it's worth understanding these visual cues. As with personality traits, body language is another great tool to help analyze other people better.

For this exercise, let's analyze some clinical studies that have focused on body language.

Facial Expressions

This is the first part of the body that you're likely to notice. Considering the face has 43 muscles that all move around as we communicate, it shows a lot is going on in our facial expressions. Don't worry, help is at hand. You can learn to 'decode' those various expressions, to give you a sense of a person's personality. You can also learn how to 'encode' your own facial movements. by doing this, you can give off the right messages that you want to convey about yourself.

The face conveys a great deal of nonverbal indicators. From the eyebrows to the laugh lines, and even how often we blink, it's all-important information for an analyst.

One researcher, Paul Ekman, believes it's all about understanding the micro-expressions. These are initial expressions that happen in around half a second. They're so quick and unconsciously performed, that they're almost impossible to fake. Ekman argued that seven key expressions are universal across the globe. No matter which country or culture you come from, you are likely to use the same expressions as someone else at the other end of the world.

These 'automatic' expressions are:

Happiness – smiling.

Sadness - frowning.

Fear - open mouth to breathe in lots of oxygen in readiness for fight or flight.

Anger – brows furrowed, nostrils dilated.

Disgust – nose wrinkled

Surprise – eyebrows raised, eyes wide.

Contempt – eyes narrowed and looking down the nose.

For the sake of analysis, these expressions give away the emotional state of a person. That's before they're able to take control of themselves consciously. It would take intense training to be able to hide your micro-expressions. Then again, it takes good training to be quick enough to read expressions too.

One other important feature of facial body language is that of eye contact. It can show the confidence, or weakness, of a person. You too can use this to convey your own confidence. Don't overdo your eye staring though. If you maintain eye contact for longer 4-5 seconds at a time, it may indicate a challenge or confrontation.

Research in Czech (K Kleisner), in 2014, studied intelligence by looks. His study showed that humans can judge the intelligence of men by their faces alone. Yet, not the intelligence of women.

Is this more a cultural and learned ability?

For instance, men with large noses are often seen as strong. Whereas a woman with a large nose may be seen as unattractive.

Is Kleisner's research showing much the same behavior?

Over time, we learn to mold our own views on how an intelligent person might look. This will likely be taken from people we meet in our lives. Or, people in the media. In the past most intelligent people were male. This is all down to the discrimination that women suffered, particularly in an academic setting.

Could this be a stereotyping of looks rather than factual?

When you find clinical studies in your research, always question the results. That is unless there is clear scientific evidence. Be open with your beliefs even when you read conflicting information. Before making your assessment, take into account some of what you read, then compare that information to other similar studies.

Can we learn to control our face so other's cannot read us?

It's often referred to as the 'poker face.' It came about from people who gamble for high rewards. They would not want competitors to read their facial expressions, so they learned how to maintain a blank face. That way, they will not give away their card hand. It's unlikely they could control pupil dilation though. This is affected by light. Instead, they may control how often they blink. Such a person will be careful about what they do with their lips. Should they bite the bottom lip, it could give away their nervousness. Their competitors may see this as a bad hand, or that they are bluffing.

The look on someone's face is so important to us and can even influence our own emotions. A study carried out in 1996 showed that if you see a person looking afraid, you are likely to feel afraid too. Of course, it's your brain at play, readying you for something dangerous that might be about to happen. What it does show, is how other people's expressions influence us.

We learn how much we can control our facial expressions according to social etiquette. For instance, if we are sad we may be showing this to others so we can get the help and attention we need. In contrast, if we are angry, it's not so acceptable so we might try to hide the expression of anger.

How can all this help you in your analysis of another person's behavior?

> ➤ By learning about facial expressions, you will be reading other people's emotions. You will be able to analyze their personality without the need to know any details about their lives.
>
> ➤ You can learn to influence others by controlling your own expressions. Observe for yourself how easily other people mirror you.
>
> ➤ Equally, mirroring other people is a great way to be accepted by them, so long as you don't overdo it.

As we grow older in life, to some extent we learn how to hide certain expressions, such as if we're wanting to tell a lie. We'll cover deceit in another chapter, but it shows how important it can be to watch facial expressions closely.

Hands and Arms

As well as giving away lots of clues with our facial expressions, we do much talking with our hands and arms too. Again, much of this is done subconsciously.

If you're preparing an important demonstration for an audience, it's well worth planning your hand and arm movements in advance. After all, you plan the words in your speech, don't you? Planning your body language could be the key difference between a powerful presentation, or a boring one.

Recent studies have found a link between how you communicate with your hands, and your intelligence. The more you use your hands, the more intelligent you may be. Hand gesturing also indicates strong leadership abilities.

BUT, it's all dependant on whether your hand movements match with the words that you're saying.

Your audience is subconsciously judging you by how you move your hands and arms when you speak. Hand movements are similar to those facial micro-expressions. A genuine hand gesture happens seconds before a speaker talks. Any hand/arm gestures following the spoken words are ones that have been thought about and calculated. A speech without any hand gestures would appear to translate as cold and wooden. If that happens, the audience is not going to trust your words. They will see a speech with hand gestures as more open and honest. Research shows that the right kind of hand gesturing can increase the impact of a speech by around 60%

There has even been research done on observing TED (Technolgy, Entertainment, and Design) speakers. These are video presentations that take 18 minutes for the speaker to get their view over to an audience. The most popular speakers used around 465 hand/arm gestures. In comparison, the least popular ones used only half of that at around 272 hand/arm gestures

Psychologist, S Kelly, Colgate University, argues that hand gesturing isn't an 'add-on' to language, it's a fundamental part of it.

We mentioned that folded arms can give off a sense of a barrier, but it's not always that simple. But, there are up to sixty different messages in a crossed arm gesture. It might be worth learning the differing interpretations so you don't get them wrong.

Some gestures are more obvious than others. Like using the thumb-up gesture to show confidence in something. Other examples are hands-on-hips and pointing your finger. All can be interpreted as a show of aggression when used in certain situations.

Negative hand/arm gestures can be used as a bullet point to stress certain words in your speech. Be careful that such gestures are not a distraction from your words. For instance:

- ➢ Closed gestures, such as crossed arms and fisted hands, are considered negative. They could create a barrier between the speaker and their audience.
- ➢ Waving your arms above your head will only serve to distract from your words. The audience will be so busy watching your negative movements that they won't be listening to you.

- Keep your hands in the acceptable box which sits between the shoulders and the waist.
- Use fluid gestures, not robotics ones. Unless you're wanting to shout out bold statements and hammer your fist in the air for a powerful punch line. You could even use a pointed finger. Another negative gesture in the wrong circumstance, but great to emphasize a point.
- Don't be afraid to use your fingers too. If a small number needs emphasizing, then put up the same amount of fingers for your audience to see. Equally, if you're emphasizing the words large or small, use your fingers or arms to show a large or small opening. The visual effect helps those listening to remember the point that you're making

In a more personal conversation, be careful how often you wave your hands and arms around. This is no longer a speech that you're making to an audience, but a more personal, intimate communication.

Open up your arms and hands to invite your listeners into your world.

The list is lengthy, and how you work your hands and arms with the rest of your body creates many different messages. For example, where you place your hand on your own body, it can give off messages too. Placing your hand close to the heart can indicate sincerity and love. Yet, a hand on the chest can show surprise or shock. What the exact message you're conveying will depend on what your eyes and face are doing at the same time.

Confused? Wait until you discover the importance of legs and feet.

Feet and Legs

As with the face, hands, and arms, your feet and legs also reveal much about our inner thoughts. While everyone's busy trying to control their upper body, they forget that their lower body needs regulating too. This is a part of the body that those trained in controlling their nonverbal language tend to forget about. It could mean that this is where we'll find the truth.

From simple movements of the foot, you can learn so much. Such as, which way the toes are pointing indicates where the person wishes they were going. If you're in a conversation and the other person's feet are pointing away from you, they're likely wishing they were somewhere else.

Feet are fairly primitive in their control. It's all down to the limbic part of the brain. This part of the brain wants quick access to your fee, in case the 'fight or flight' action is needed. What this means is that before you've even got around to concentrating on what your lower body is doing, your brain has automatically done it for you. Hence, if you don't want to be with someone, before you realize it, your brain is sending messages for your foot to point in a getaway direction.

The next time you see a politician saying all the right words and doing all the corresponding upper body movements, take a look at his lower body. That's where you'll know if they're being honest, once you learn to read the right body language.

The position of our legs also says much about us. Did you know that when you cross your legs, 70% will favor the left over the right leg? This is regardless of whether they're left or right-handed.

Let's have a look at the meaning of some arm and leg positions:

- If someone is sitting down and bouncing a knee or foot up and down, they're either nervous or impatient for a quick getaway.

- Whether our legs are open or closed can be down to gender, but it could also be about what's going on in our minds. Someone standing with their legs slightly apart looks, and feels, dominant. Whereas someone standing with their legs crossed will be looked upon as weaker.

- If a person's legs and arms are crossed at the same time, it could indicate that their mind is elsewhere. They're not interested in what's going on around them.

- Oh, and be careful about showing off the soles of your feet because in some cultures this is an insult. The bottom of the feet are associated with the filth on the floor.

There are so many ways to cross the legs and all give off different messages. To complicate it further, there are gender differences too.

- For instance, there are positions of leg crossing that are acceptable for women but may be seen as weak in a man. Men tend to use the figure-four to cross their legs, keeping their knees apart. The figure-four is also a stance that might show the person is a little self-opinionated and hasn't got a great deal of respect for the people around them.

- If a man is sitting with his legs open fairly wide, then he's indicating how viral he is. He's confident, and even a little smug.

We'll give you one more example as for food for thought, because this section could fill a book on its own.

- When a woman slips her foot in and out of her shoe, it reminds any male who's observing her of the actions of intercourse. He might be sitting there with vivid and passionate thoughts rampaging through his head. So, be careful girls who you're swinging your shoe at.

The advice might be to keep your feet firmly on the floor and point your toes in front. Then again, that may make you look a little stiff ad giving off an uncaring message. The truth is, your feet and legs need to be doing different things in different situations. You don't want them too relaxed at an interview but you do if you're on a date. If you can remember to point your feet at the person you're talking to, that may be enough to convince them that you're listening.

Then again, what are your face and your hands telling them? It's not easy, is it?

Body Posture

Let's move on from limbs and look at what the body as a whole might be saying. Your poise and posture say a great deal about who you are and how you feel.

We can use examples from the animal kingdom that will help us understand the power play in posture. If you want to appear dominant and powerful, then it helps if you can make yourself appear larger. Much like the silverback gorilla does to intimidate his competitors. Even if you don't feel that powerful, you can still give the impression that you are. Once you manage it, other people's behavior should be more positive towards you.

One theory is that it takes only 2 minutes for your body to start pumping those powerhouse hormones. Then you should feel confident and energized, as follows:

- As you use a power stance you will feel good about yourself.
- This results in your body pumping all the right hormones, such as adrenalin.
- Now your brain will influence your behavior, making you more self-confident.
- So...get it right!

To learn more about other people's behavior you will need to observe them. Try sitting in a park as you do this. Don't concentrate on their faces or limbs, observe how they move their body as a whole. For instance -

How do they sit, stand, and walk?

Are their shoulders back, or slouching forward?

Do they look stiff, or relaxed?

Which way does their body turn if they're talking with another person?

All the above will give you clues about the emotions of the people you are observing. You don't even need to know what anyone is talking about. In your stance, it's all about how open, or closed, your body language is.

Here are some examples.

Standing

How you stand, if you do it right, can make you feel more confident.

- Loosen the arms and keep them relaxed. No crossing them or fidgeting with fingers or hands. For more advice on how to use your arms and hands, go back to that section in this book.

- Use your head to look tall. Get into the habit of holding your chin up a little. If you find your head drooping, lift that chin and push back a little with your neck, (this also helps to get rid of a double-chin). NO drooping heads, chins, or shoulders allowed.

- Use those shoulders to make yourself look big, even if you're a woman. Women can be as dominant as men. If you want to be among the alphas in the room, then you need that high power pose to ward off your competitors.

- Use your legs too. Keep your feet apart about 4 inches as you align your legs with the edges of your shoulders. Any power pose should be relaxed and open. If you stand rigid, it may have the complete opposite effect on your audience.

- Take into account personal space when judging how close to stand next to other people. Personal space is important. If you infiltrate it, all that hard work on your posture is wasted. As a rule of thumb, stand between 2-4 feet away from people you don't know too well. Inside of the 2ft zone is the intimate area, so learn to judge distances.

- The opposite of a high power pose is a low power pose. This is when you make yourself look small as if you don't want anyone to notice you. It can give off a message of weakness and a lack of self-confidence.

Power Pose In Summary,

- Whilst you don't want to be rude, take up as much space as you can.
- Make sure all your limbs are unlocked.
- Hold your chin up.
- Smile with your mouth and your eyes.
- That should win everyone over.

Sitting

Your posture, as you sit down, can be influenced by your mood and environment. For instance, you're hardly likely to put your feet up on the table at a Board meeting, but you might when you're in the office. Different positions for differing moods and situations.

Here's a brief guide of a few seated positions and how you can analyze their meaning:

- People who sit-up straight tend to have good self-confidence. It takes effort to hold everything in place, such as your back and shoulders. They're making a conscious attempt to look tall. This could be considered a power pose. If they appear too stiff though, then it can give a sense of unapproachability.

- Cross the tops of your legs and you could be feeling less confident about yourself. Then again, if you only cross your ankles, this gives off the opposite message.

- Those who sit crossed-legged on the floor, tend to look quite relaxed. For some though, this could be an impossible position for health reasons. Those who sit on the floor with their arms leaning back are showing that they're observers. Watch out because they're watching you watching them.

- Are you an armrest clutcher when sitting in a chair that has arms? If your hands are grabbing hard at them, then ask yourself what's going on in your mind? Are you uncomfortable with your surroundings? Try and relax your grip so your anxiety levels settle down too.

- Crossing arms and legs to protect your body, like a barrier, can mean much the same whether standing or sitting. This person is uncomfortable with their surroundings or situation. If you find yourself doing this, open up a bit and you'll feel more relaxed.

- Then there is where you chose to position yourself on a park bench or even in a room full of people. Do you head for the middle, or the edges? Those who throw themselves in the middle are confident and want to show their presence.

- Someone attempting to hide their hands away could also be hoping not to be noticed. It's another barrier that shows they're uncomfortable with their situation.

As you can see, the message a person gives off as they sit down tells many a secret. Even how they position their arms, hands, legs, and feet. If that foot is pointing away from the person they're talking to, they could want out of the conversation. If it's pointing towards someone, then they're comfortable with the person they're conversing with.

Walking

Want to look confident while walking? Then take larger strides to show that you're a confident person and sure of your destination. Hold your chin up slightly when walking to avoid stooping, which is not good for your frame. Fast walkers tend to be more extravert in their character, unless they're in a rush of course. These are the drivers in life. They want to get where they're going, and fast, and that tends to be their outlook for everything.

> ➢ Avoid walking with your head down if you can. It could mean you're avoiding face to face contact with other people, even if you're not aware of it. Here's a trick to help you with this

one. If you don't like eye contact with the people who pass you by, focus on another part of their upper body, such as their arms. That should help you avoid any unwelcome stares.

- Someone who stamps their feet hard on the ground as they walk is giving signals that they may have a temper. If they drag their feet, it can indicate they are lethargic and even anxious or depressed.
- Those with a smooth swagger to their gait tend to be great socializers. This type of person may use exaggerated hand gestures and focus on the here and now.
- As with all body movements, the more open and wide your gait, the more confident and friendly you appear.

As with sitting and standing, those shoulders are giving away secrets too.

Shoulders

The saying of, "bearing the weight of the world on your shoulders," indicates you're carrying a lot of emotional baggage. It comes from Greek mythology in the clash of Titans. The god, Atlas, was condemned to stand at the edge of the world and hold the sky upon his shoulders. So, to "lift the weight from your shoulders," has the opposite effect. You are now relieved of your burdens. Such bold statements show how we use the shoulders as a symbol of strength.

Those of us who are shy and introvert, tend to slump the shoulders down, along with the head. This way, they are protecting the throat too, which is a vulnerable area of the body. By pushing the chest forward a little, and raising the chin a little, it straightens the shoulders better. You're also leaving your throat open, which indicates you don't feel the need to protect yourself. A great power pose.

Appearance

In this section let's consider a person's appearance, or rather their personal image. The clothes you wear, your hair, make up, and accessories, they all play a part in building up your personal identity.

A man wearing a suit and tie may be considered classy, as well as formal. How well-tailored his suit is, will also play its part. If it's well-tailored and expensive, he may be looked upon as wealthy, and a man of good taste.

Your clothes demonstrate a lot about who you are. As we have already discussed, your personality alters with age, so too will the clothes that you wear. Many of us strive for the top fashions in our teenage years. As we age, we're less influenced by brand names. At this point in our lives, we tend to wear clothes that are comfortable rather than fashionable. On that note, your clothes can give away your age, not only your physical age but also the age you feel.

We all tend to follow certain unspoken social dress codes.

- Formal wear in the office.
- Elegant wear at a wedding, or party.
- Uniforms at school, and for certain careers such as police officers or nursing.
- Even different cultures enforce certain dress codes upon us.

It's what we do with our outfit that can give away even more of those little tell-tale signs. For instance:

Take our man who's wearing a suit and tie. Should he undo his tie and top shirt button then he's no longer considered formal. Now, he's giving off a message that he's more relaxed. Which is fine once the working day, or conference he's attending, is over. What might be odd, is if he did that in the middle of a Board meeting. Such behavior with the clothing would now be considered ignorant and rude.

This emphasizes how we have invented our own unwritten rules on dress code.

Your attire can give off so much information to those who observe human behavior. Even to the point of the accessories that you choose to wear.

- ➢ We may consider someone who wears a lot of jewelry as needing to show off that they're attractive, or wealthy. They are conscious of themselves and care what others think about them.

- ➢ In contrast, someone who wears little jewelry doesn't feel the need to show off their wealth. They feel confident enough about themselves without lots of accessories.

- Even how you wear your glasses, if you wear them, can give away messages. If you peer over the lenses to look at another person, it could indicate that you're being critical of them. You might find the other person crosses their arms back at you because that's what they sense. It's all in the little details.

It's much the same with make-up that women wear.

- Too much and they may be considered extravagant or even sassy. These people are attention seekers.
- Those wearing more subtle make-up want to be seen as attractive.

There are so many different messages other people are receiving about us based purely on the way we look. Though, what that message says also depends on the personality of the perceiver.

For instance, take our example of women and makeup. Those who wear no make-up at all could be seen as:

- Unattractive.
- Lazy, because they can't be bothered.

> Or, are they confident enough in themselves that they don't care what others think?

In that example alone, you have three different views of how other people are perceiving a woman who's not wearing make-up. Throw a spanner in the works and put that make-up on a man and everyone's views will change. We humans are complex creatures, aren't we?

We are all being judged by our behavior, our movements, and what we wear. The list of non-verbal communications is endless. Here's a few more to ponder on:

> Do you smoke? If so, how do hold your cigarette? How do you blow out the smoke from your cigarette?
> How do you hold a pen?
> How do you wear sunglasses?
> How baggy or tight is your clothing?
> How expensive or cheap is your clothing?
> What type of dog do you own?

Make your own list and research what all the different interpretations might mean. It's a great way to analyze people.

Chapter 6

DARK PSYCHOLOGY

We have already discussed the 5 model personality traits of OCEAN, to help analyze people. However, there is another model that includes the darker side of psychology. This shows some of the negative aspects of certain characters. Whilst we may all have such adverse traits in small amounts, some people are ruled by them. This includes characteristics that are considered more socially unacceptable, such as dishonesty manipulation, and controlling traits.

As an example consider the serial killer Ted Bundy. This is a character who justified his murders with unreasonable beliefs. In his opinion, one less person on the earth would make no difference. Such an attitude shows that he didn't view people as important individuals. In comparison, Anne Franke, a victim of the holocaust era, had completely differing views. She believed, after all the horrors she had witnessed, that most people were good at heart. Here are two very contrasting types of personalities.

The concept of dark psychology is that we all have a dark and a light side to our personality. Why do people enjoy watching horror movies? It's the thirst of their darker side attempting to satisfy an odd craving. One research in 2013, Jones and Figuerido, explains the likes of Ted Bundy. They showed that at the heart of dark traits lay antagonistic characteristics. Such traits will include callous behavior.

For most of us, our dark side is nothing more than morbid curiosity. Some may slow down whilst driving, to look at a road accident. Others may enjoy playing violent computer games. All serving to satisfy our darker appetite but with no harm done to anyone but ourselves.

For some though, this isn't enough. They have a deep need to take their cravings to the extreme. Such people may seem normal on the outside, at first. On the inside, they are seething with aggressive thoughts. Such cravings eventually come out as violent behavior against others. At its most extreme, some can enjoy giving, and even receiving pain. These darker traits are all about power and control.

The Dark Triad

Psychological studies have come up with The Dark Triad. It runs along with the same principles as the Big Five Personality Traits: OCEAN. The difference is that the Dark Triad looks at the more negative aspects of a personality. Though it is also based on nature and nurture influences. To calculate the extent of a person's darker side, they would need to complete a personality test. Such tests are often used to evaluate psychiatric patients. They are even used in law to assess unstable criminals. More innocently, they are also used by bigger corporations to assess future employees.

In the Dark Triad there are three main traits:

Narcissism

A narcissist has a high sense of self-importance. This will be to the point of feeling superior over everyone else around them. They believe they are dominant and enjoy egotistical behavior. It's not so much that they are intentional deceivers. More to the point is that they convince themselves their lies are the truth. This type of personality can be extrovert, and even creative. Their social skills are often poor and they may overcompensate by being doing every task excessively.

Machiavellianism

This type of trait is only interested in their personal gains in life. They will deceive others on purpose, if only to gain what they believe is theirs by rights. This is the manipulator who will go to any lengths to gain personal rewards.

Psychopathy

Of the three main traits, this has the strongest evidence that it is inherited through genes in the chromosomes. A psychopath has a cruel streak running through everything they believe. It can become more extreme as they age. Psychopaths will be bold and uncaring, prepared to hurt anyone, or anything, that gets in their way. This is an impulsive character who shows extreme determination and callousness to get what they want.

None of the darker traits are acceptable norms. Those who display them tend to lack empathy, and moral values. Their behavior is deceitful, manipulative, and controlling. In studies, men have been more prone to such toxic behavior, than women. There is a link with the chemical hormones too, such as testosterone. They will be the first to impose punishments on others who break the social rules. Yet, they will be blind to their own antisocial conduct.

One study observed people with such personalities as they were shown images of faces. The results showed that they experienced joy at seeing images of unhappy faces. Yes, when presented with happy faces, they all showed a certain degree of disappointment. Those diagnosed with narcissism and psychopathy experienced pleasure at seeing angry faces. The more frightening result came from those diagnosed with psychopathy. They expressed enjoyment when shown faces that looked fearful.

Such people can do well in their careers. They may even reach high levels, but it may often be short-lived. It can be difficult to keep their behavior under control. Jonason and colleagues (2012) found strong differences in such traits in the workplace. The narcissist will be keen to wear superior attire and enjoy dressing as a leader. Machiavellians will use excessive faux charm in their leadership role. The psychopath will utilize bullying to climb the ladder of success.

How can you identify people with such toxic personality traits?

Typically, they will be bullies, such as:

- ➢ Internet trolls
- ➢ People with racist values.
- ➢ Those who show antisocial behavior.
- ➢ Those who show aggressive behavior and lean towards violence as the answer to everything.
- ➢ Some may only show such behavior in private and be the perfect epitome of charm in public.
- ➢ If they do have a sexual partner, they may be excessively possessive.
- ➢ They may even enjoy taking other people's partners away from them. Once they have succeeded, the game is over as they become bored and disregard their prize.

Traits of the Dark Triad Personality

This book is about analyzing other people. That includes those, who through no fault of their own, end up in a relationship with a manipulative or abusive partner. By understanding the darker traits of this type of personality, you might be able to avoid allowing such people into your life.

A manipulative person has a very controlling personality. They may think nothing of being aggressive, and even violent. Such people tend to think it is their right to hurt those who 'belong' to them. Yes, that's how they see their victims, as their 'property'.

Dark psychology shows how unethical some people are willing to behave so they can get what they want. Such people will never feel remorse. That's because they lack the emotions to experience any regret over making other people suffer. They may even find it fun to see other people's pain. Are they ill? Well, that's under much scientific debate but it's hard to lay blame when, as we have shown, we are all running on genes and hormones. But, living with such a person can be a shattering experience for the victim.

How to avoid being the victim of such a relationship?

We can all act a little selfish and manipulative to get what we want. We may be guilty of exaggerating our strengths in an interview. Or, bending the truth a little if we're in a tight spot. It's something we all do in an almost evolutionary way. You could say it's a form of survival to improve our life chances. It's only when it harms others that it is bordering on the darker traits.

First of all, such a person's mind works in different ways. To them, the darker traits are their norm. They won't see their cruel behavior as wrong, they will see what they do as necessary for their own survival. Isn't that how we all think anyway? It's a hard call!

Such people, most especially if you find them sexually attractive, will be very charming at the beginning of any friendship. They want to impress their victims. They say that 'we are blinded by love,' and this so often appears to be true. Other people may tell you that your new partner is a 'bad' person. Yet, you are blinded by your own infatuation, and it can be hard for them to convince you otherwise. After all, this new person in your life is going out of their way to make you feel good.

Let's have a look at some of the tell-tale signs of a person with strong dark traits ruling their personality.

Vulnerable Victims

Manipulative predators usually home in on vulnerable people. They don't have a strong constitution themselves, so they have a great need to control a weaker person. A controlling manipulator will take advantage of your weaknesses. They will continue to exploit such weaknesses until they have total power over you.

Their ideal victim may be:

- Lonely, without much in the way of close family and friends.
- Gone through a bad experience, such as divorce or death, and may have inherited money.
- Elderly.
- Unhealthy.
- Young and naive.
- Shy and introvert.

If you're in the unfortunate situation of living with someone like this, they will want to:

- Control your every move.
- Control all the finances.
- Decide who you can and can't be friends with.

Watch out for the signs. Their impeccable manners and amazing charms will not last forever. Take your time before you let this person into your life. If they grow impatient, let them go before they ensnare you. If you can spot such behavior in time, you can move on from such an unhealthy relationship.

Of course, not all people with manners and charm are manipulators. A genuine person will be patient and allow you time to take things at your own pace. You will know this person because you won't feel under any pressure. They will give you space, which is very important in a healthy relationship.

Personal Space

Be extra careful of a person who constantly invades your private space. They will overstep your boundaries because they can. You may not even notice it at first, as they charm their way into your life. Such a character may smother you with their protective wing. Except it's not to protect you, it's to lure you into their prison of ownership.

Domineering Behavior

Possessiveness

Once they feel they have total control over you, their jealous nature will start to shine through. If someone insists that you don't go out with your friends anymore, or see your relatives, be careful. Your social world is getting smaller as their possession of you gets tighter. They will create a barrier making other's feel unwelcome. Although they may also allow those in who they feel they can control.

Opinionated

If your new partner believes they are right all the time, in every view they have, tread carefully. Do they refuse to listen to other people's opinions and then speak to others with condescension in their tone? They may even ridicule others, at every opportunity. That's because it gives them a sordid pleasure to see others in emotional turmoil. If your partner behaves in this way, you may begin to question your own judgment. Your self-esteem will take a downwards spiral as their grip strengthens.

Aggressive Attitude

Do you find your new friend constantly rolling their eyes at you?

Do they 'tut' at everything you do?

Do they embarrass you in public, making you look a pathetic fool?

Beware, this is the beginnings of classic controlling behavior.

Their true nature is shining through. This disapproval of you will only get stronger and more frequent. It may even turn to aggression as they become impatient with you. Eventually, they may use violence if you don't behave how they want you to. Once went out of their way to please you. Now, they wish only to make you miserable, because they get pleasure from that.

If you try to rally against them, they may use the tactic of making you feel guilty for doubting them. They could accuse you of hurting their feelings. The more you are ensnared, the quicker their respect for you disperses. Woe betide you, though, if you don't show them respect!

Such a person has very little patience and when things don't go their way, they could lash out. That lashing will be coming your way as they will see everything that goes wrong as your fault. And now the bullying begins. It's not unusual for a victim to suffer physical, mental, and sexual abuse from a manipulative partner.

After they've hurt their victims, some will go out of their way to apologize and promise it won't happen ever again. Others may accuse you of unreasonable behavior and claim you brought it upon yourself. In the end, you'll be exhausted, emotionally drained, and confused. The only thing you can be certain of is that it will happen again, and again, and again. It's all an act!

You can never satisfy the underlying selfishness and greed of such a person. They are incapable of accepting that they are bad. If anything, they most likely believe they are the best thing in your life. It's up to you to make that decision, not them!

How do you escape a controlling relationship?

By analyzing other people's behavior, you can learn to differentiate manipulation from persuasion. When someone attempts to make you do something, and the only person who benefits from it is them, they are manipulating you. If the act is to benefit yourself, then it is not manipulation but more likely persuasion. They are offering you genuine advice.

Partnership

It's important first, to admit to yourself that you are in an unhealthy relationship. Is your partner, or friend, self-opinionated, selfish, and overbearing? If they are aggressive and violent, it's time to leave them behind and move on without them. The chances are they are controlled by the darker traits. If your partner's behavior falls into the darker traits, then the chances are they cannot change. This would take a long time and only with professional help.

If you're in this type of relationship, the chances are that you've been putting up with their controlling behavior for a long time. You may even fear them and feel unsure how to break free. It's not easy to leave them when they live in your home. What can make it even more difficult is if they are the biological parent to your child/ren. Such factors make the decision to leave them seem impossible.

Of course, it's not only partnerships of this sort you need to avoid. Keep anyone that is driven by the darker traits out of your life. For instance, do you think you have a control freak at your place of employment? if so, then do your best to avoid them. Deal with them only when you have to because the contact is work-related.

Gaslighting

If you've been in a long term relationship with someone ruled by dark traits, they are most likely 'gaslighting' you. It means that your partner, or friend, works on your weaknesses to the point that you feel like the guilty party. For instance:

They'll convince you that whenever something goes wrong, it's your doing. Even going out of their way to make you believe that's the truth.

With their devious ways, they'll make you feel incompetent, inadequate, and pretty darn useless.

Standing up to them may cause them to become abusive, and you know better than to take that course of action. Though, if your partner is abusive then you are suffering from domestic violence. Later, we will look at where you can find help to leave such a relationship.

Domestic Violence

Let's first take a look at the different forms of domestic violence.

In the US, around 20 people a minute (around 10million people), suffer abuse from an intimidating partner.

Have a look at the following typical behavior traits, and see if any of them seem similar to your own partner/friend.

- ➤ They control ALL the finances, leaving you very little money, even if you work.
- ➤ They have angry outbursts, such as punching, or throwing items around. This can lead to them hitting out at you too.
- ➤ They blame everyone else for their problems, but mostly you.
- ➤ They stop you from seeing your friends and family, isolating you.
- ➤ They tell you how to dress. Sometimes they even make fun of you by belittling you in front of other people.
- ➤ If you try to leave them, they may threaten you with violence. Or, they may go the other way and tell you that they can't live without you, so they will commit suicide.

All of this emotional, and physical, turmoil can lead to your own personality and health changes, such as:

> ➢ Low self-esteem, even though you used to be confident.

> ➢ Constant anxiety and depression, as you never know what mood they'll be in.

> ➢ Missing work because they've bruised you.

> ➢ Problems getting a good night's sleep because you lay awake worrying. This can also lead to suffering terrible headaches.

How can you take action?

ADMIT THERE IS A PROBLEM!

First, you need to understand and accept that you are NOT to blame. In fact, no one is to blame, as the perpetrator may not be able to help themselves. That is no reason to take pity on them. For your own well being, you must plan a course of action to get out of such an unhealthy situation.

Start to make plans as soon as you can. Try not to act any differently than usual. This will be difficult but you don't want to give off any hints of your future plans. It can be difficult to find friends and family to help you because your partner may have forced you to sever ties with them.

You don't need to do any of this alone. Why not involve someone who can help you? There are people who deal with such problems all the time. They're experienced in understanding what you're going through. Finding them is not difficult. Begin with researching online, if you can get such an opportunity. You are looking to build up a support network, such as agencies that can support you:

- The Domestic Violence Resource Center.
- The Office of Women's Health.
- The National Domestic Violence Hotline.
- Battered Women's Justice Project.
- Violence Against Women.

These are but a few of the agencies who help people in your situation, there are many more, and they're not only for women. Look for local ones, as they may have a safe-house for you to go live in for a while.

Delete the searches on your computer or phone if you're frightened your partner will find out. It's important not to give away any clues on what you are planning. Sneaking away might not sound fair, but swallow your pride. If you've got this far then you've accepted that your partner/friend is not good for you.

Coping Strategies

There are strategies to help you cope, while you're still in the stressful situation of making your escape plan. Here are a few:

Journal

While you're going through the hard times, one great mental health exercise is to write a journal. By writing down your thoughts, you are detaching yourself from the bad experience. Look at your words later, and allow yourself to feel emotional. If you are with a violent partner, the chances are that you bottle up all your feelings. Take this moment to let those emotions come to the surface. This is a private space to jot everything down that happens to you on a daily basis. It's time for you to gather your thoughts and emotions. Your journal not meant to be read by anyone but you, so put it somewhere safe. The last thing you need is for a manipulative partner to find it.

Breathing Techniques

Learn how to use relaxation breathing to help with the stressful times when you're alone. Breathing techniques are simple to learn.

- ➢ Take a deep breath in, allowing your tummy to expand so you take in plenty of oxygen to your lungs.
- ➢ Hold it for a count of around 4.
- ➢ Let the breath out slowly.

Some people prefer to intake the air through their nose and exhale through an open mouth. Do whatever is the easiest method for you. Keep repeating until you feel the tension has eased. It works better than counting to 10, which only serves to take your mind away from what's happening. Breathing techniques help to relax your whole body.

Relaxation Positions

When you get a moment to yourself, lay flat on your back on the floor, sofa, or bed, with your arms lose and down by your sides.

- ➢ Close your eyes and perform a few deep breathing sessions before you begin.

- Focus your mind on your toes, and wiggle them.
- Next - Think about your ankles, and twirl them.

The idea is to move up your body with your thoughts. Focus on different parts of your body, such as muscles in the back of your shins, knees, thighs, bottom, hips, and onwards and upwards. Squeeze the muscles when you get to them, and then relax them. Rotate, or move, joints around, such as the ankles, knees, wrists, and shoulders.

As you work your way through your body, focus on nothing but the task in hand. By the time you complete the whole body, you should feel more relaxed.

Other ways that can help with relaxation, vary for different people. Some like to listen to music, or escape with a good book. We all need to find ways of relaxing that help us unwind. Mental health is as important as physical health. Give your mind a break and find some activity that helps it close down, if only for half an hour.

Once you can admit that you need help, you will be opening the door to freedom. It will not be an easy journey but it will be a worthwhile one. Now the door is open, all you have you have to do is step through it and come out at the other side. Once through, you may feel afraid of being alone, but allow yourself time to recover. Don't rush into any new relationships because you need time to heal from the hurt and pain that you've gone through.

The Legacy of Abuse

Abusive adults cannot always blame dark personality traits. It's well documented that children who suffer abuse can often turn into the abusers, later in life. Though, not all experts agree with this. A recent study, (Kaufman and Zigler), showed that only a third of this group will turn into abusers. Yet other such studies appear to be in conflict with this belief. (R Krugman), showed that a high proportion of adult abusers were abused themselves. Krugman revealed there are key factors that will affect whether the abused turns into the abuser. Here are some examples:

- ➢ How young a person is when the abuse occurs.
- ➢ The length of time the abuse goes on for. Abuse does not need to be harrowing to leave mental scarring. Repeated abuse can do this too.

- Who the perpetrator is, ie family or nonfamily member. If it is a family member, the victim may suffer trust issues of loved ones, later in life.

- Whether or not the child perceived the abuse as wrong or acceptable. If the child doesn't see the abusive behavior as wrong, this is where problems arise. Such children may consider that being beaten with a belt as an acceptable punishment because that's what their parents have taught them. This creates a denial in their young minds. Those who deny their abuse are more likely to become the abusers, as they see such behavior as the norm. They will grow up with a distorted view of what is normal and what is unacceptable. Such a confused mind may well repeat the behavior, only this time as the abuser.

- The atmosphere in the family, ie cold and uncaring, or warm and loving. This last factor plays a major role on how the child copes with the abuse. Loving support can help victims overcome many of life's traumas.

One study disclosed that recovery is more related to the after-support a victim receives. If the parents/carers provided love and support, the victim may, in time, learn to put the experience behind them. If they don't have that support mechanism in place, the child may go on to feel unwanted. A child without nurturing support is more likely to become an abusive adult. Such adults can go on to suffer terrible mental health issues. Even to the point of developing personality disorders, such as multiple personalities. Such disorders can stem from how the abused child attempted to deal with the horrors done to them. One such study, 1985, showed that of 15 adolescents convicted of murder, 13 of them had been victims of horrendous abuse as young children.

The cold nature of a parent/carer can leave any child traumatized. One such study found that:

- ➢ An abused child, with caring parents, suffers little mental illness.
- ➢ An unharmed child, whose parents show little emotional care, suffer higher mental anxieties.

Extreme mental abuse is as harmful as physical abuse, in a child. It can lead the victim to suffer neurological damage. This can include distressful headaches, memory loss, and even diminished mental abilities.

Thankfully, not all abused children become abusive adults. One study, (Hunt), showed that the child who accepts they were abused is more likely to be treatable. This is the child who understands that what happened to them was wrong. This is the child that will hopefully grow into a well-balanced adult, despite their terrible experience.

How to Detect a Lie

The final part of our exploration into the darker side of the personality traits looks at how to tell when other people are lying to you. Studies show that around 80% of lies remain undetected, so it can be useful to learn how to spot a lie. Body language plays an important role in this.

When people lie, there are subtle changes in their brain activity. Other people cannot see this, but they can see the results of it. Increasing stress levels caused by lying will release chemicals, such as cortisol. This causes the brain's temperature to rise. The result of this will create those tell-tale micro-body movements that can give away so many secrets. The most obvious can be a sudden light sheen of sweat upon the brow or a flushing face. Nonverbal cues are the key tell-tale signs to look out for, unless someone has trained long and hard to avoid giving themselves away,

Some people claim they never lie! Well, that is a big fat lie, to begin with. A social psychology study resulted in showing that 60% of people will lie on average, every 10 minutes. Another study indicated that we each of us tell around 11 lies a week. *Are these studies, indeed, lying?*

Most of us only tell what we call little white lies. It could be to avoid something embarrassing or to stop others from judging their behavior. Have you ever avoided a meeting by saying you were ill when you were quite well but didn't want to go? Or, have you complimented someone's new dress when you thought it looked terrible? Harmless enough, but once nonetheless, all lies. Once you learn that those little lies can be useful, it can be a slippery slope with a snowballing effect. The more our lies become undetected, the more likely we are to lie again, and again. When you combine the ease at which most of us lie, and also how easy it is to dupe other people, you can see why we may all be living under an avalanche of untruths. Research shows that those mistrustful statements are only discovered 53% of the time. So, there's a fifty-fifty chance of being discovered, or not!

Want to know whether someone is telling you the truth or not? Then observe their behavior rather than listen to what they are telling you. This is where knowing a person's "baseline behavior," which we discussed earlier in the book, becomes useful. Technically, it should be easier to spot a mistruth in someone you know. That's because you'll be used to their baseline behavior. For others who you don't know, well, "the windows are the eyes to the soul," so they say. *Is that a portal to the truth?* Well, kind of, but here are a few other nonverbal signs to look out for:

- Flaring nostrils. They may be mad at you because you've found them out.
- Biting lips. Subconsciously worrying that you might know that they're lying.
- Fast blinking, unless that's the norm for them.
- Avoiding eye contact, or even the opposite of staring at you. This depends on what their normal baseline behavior is like. If someone is lying, they'll often do the opposite of their baseline. Experts can even look for dilation of the

pupils, though this is more difficult in an everyday situation.

- Changing the tone of voice, such as higher or lower pitch, or speaking faster or slower than normal.

- Speaking nonsense with a flustering voice, or repeating words.

- If your partner doesn't buy you gifts as a rule, and they start to buy them for you, be wary! They could be trying to hide their guilt, such as having an affair.

- Look out for those 25-second micro expressions! Hard to spot but nonetheless they are the great giveaways. The bigger the lie, or, the more guilt they feel, the more micro-expressions they tend to use.

- The false smile can be a real giveaway too. If there are no crow's feet around the eyes but they're smiling, they're most likely lying.

- Shifty eyes that move around because they don't want to look at you. Then again be careful of this one. If you don't know their baseline behavior, it could be that they're shy or nervous, so read between the lines.

➢ *What about tapping feet and knees, or the fidgeting of hands and twirling of hair? Are they all a sign of lying?* They could be, if this is not a part of their normal baseline behavior. Fidgeting hands may even touch the face. *Are they trying to cover up their face because they feel that their lie is written all over their expressions?*

You can now see how understanding someone's baseline behavior is so important. Do some good observations before you go accusing your loved ones of lying. If their behavior appears different, then it's a warning sign that something's wrong. They're under stress for some reason, so it's worth investigating. It may not be a lie, but something that's worrying them.

So, how do we deal with another person's dishonesty? Well, the chances are that the lie is a call for help. Whether it's something small or large, doesn't matter. Don't go shouting at them yet! Learn to be more empathic towards other people's needs, it's a great trait to have. Even if it doesn't come naturally, you can learn to become this person. We discuss this in our section on "changing your personality.' Mind you, don't pretend that you want to help them if you don't. They might discover you don't mean it, and find out your own little white lie!

Chapter 7

CULTURES AND BELIEFS

The environment/s we are raised in, as a child, will have a great influence on our behavior. This is the side of our personality that's affected by nurture. Part of what influences our personality will come from our main caregivers' behavior and attitude towards life. Cultural beliefs pass down through generations, so they will most likely have the same beliefs as their parents before them. Cultural beliefs have a very strong influence in tight-knit families and communities.

Religion and Behavior

For a culture to develop, there does not need to be a religion. Culture is about the group's beliefs in many things, such as food, clothing, and even music. But, the greatest influencing factor on community culture is religion.

It's been estimated, by scholars, that there are 4200 active religions throughout the world. Although there are only between 12-20 major religions. The others tend to be offshoots from the main ones. Religious groups tend to live within the same neighborhoods. It's not unusual to have several different religions in any given area. Whether they get along with one another will most likely depend on the community leaders' personalities. With good leadership, they will tolerate each other's different beliefs. With an intolerant leader, then the whole group will follow likewise.

Take a community of farmworkers and mix them with a community of city workers, will they behave differently? If they have the same religious beliefs, they may well have the same cultural beliefs. With this in common, the likelihood is that they will eat similar foods and behave in similar ways. Okay, so they may get along well together. If they are from different religious groups, they are more likely to enjoy different things with regards to food, clothing, and music. These two groups may struggle to get along with each other. Not because their work background is in different places, but because of their different religious, and cultural beliefs. It shows how strong the influence of religion is upon our cultural beliefs.

Although, cultural beliefs can evolve over time, as basic beliefs change with modernization. One example of this is the law passed in 2017 in Saudi Arabia, making it legal for women to be able to drive.

Our tolerance of each other, ie different religions living within the same neighborhood, is not always strong. Different religious groups often end up behaving antagonistically towards each other. Is the blame down to cultural beliefs, or personality traits? Certainly, an open-minded person will be more tolerant of their neighbor's different beliefs. But, communities build up a kind of herding-behavior with their cultural beliefs. In the end, it's not down to individual behavior, but more based upon the groups' cultural beliefs as a whole. The worst of it is that religion is accountable for most of the wars and hatred in our world.

Religion has been around as long as mankind. Without a doubt, cultural beliefs have a strong influence on the development of our personality.

What of technological advancements? How has that altered our behavior?

Social Media and Desensitization

Most of the human population are reasonably intelligent beings. If not in academic intelligence, at least in common sense. Yet, we can hate one another with such a vengeance, if they seem "different" from us. Why we are fueled with such passion is the cause of many ongoing philosophical discussions among academia and the sciences. It's not that we have grown less tolerance over time. There are plenty of recorded bloody historical battles between cultures and religions.

In modern times we no longer fight with axes and swords upon the battlefield. Most of our arguments happen around technology. The innovation of humans has caused many unhappy communities over history. Consider the Luddites, losing their jobs because of new machines. Or, native Indians losing their lands because of ships bringing people from other lands. The invention of the motor car and trains altered society in a big way. Horses became redundant and agricultural societies changed into factory workers.

It seems that with technology comes even more hatred. Yet technology is also the cause of more isolation. Does this mean that community life is changing?

We play on our computers and cell phones almost in an anonymous capacity. Many people act completely out of character when they can hide behind anonymity. Is humanity becoming more and more desensitized with social media? Are we caring less for the problems of those who are less fortunate than ourselves? Social media has opened up access to information. We now know of things that happen at the other side of the world, and even on other planets and in space. The data we have access to through information is vast. Yet, do we seek to better our lot? If anything, we seek more thrills and excitement through our technology.

Psychological studies show that we all have a darker side to our nature, no matter what our beliefs are. Past clinical studies have proven the darker side of humanity to be all too clear.

The classic Milgram experiment is a perfect example. It showed how people were willing to perform terrible things on other people. Normal people were led to believe that they were physically electrocuting their victims. As long as an authoritative figure gave them orders or permission to do so, very few questioned the act. Not needing to shoulder the responsibility, they desensitized themselves to their dark deeds. It was someone else's fault that they were causing pain to other people. Someone permitted them and told them to do it! It's much like being a soldier. It's okay to kill the enemy because their superiors have told them to do it?

There is certainly some dynamic at work here, and it makes you wonder about how the human brain works. Perfectly innocent people can turn into monsters. Look at how some people switch on the aggressive side of their personality when driving a car. Is nowhere safe from the ranting and raving of humans?

Let's finish this section with an example of the dark side of our personality shining through on social media. For example, take a social platform such as Facebook. Most of the posts that show up time and again are calculated to do so by using algorithms. These are the popular posts that the general public has shown the most interest in. It means many people have read and 'liked or 'commented' on them. The shocking result is that the most popular posts are the bad ones. It is us, the people, who are feeding those algorithms by making them popular. The negative stuff generates more interest than the nicer posts of fluffy cats. What does this say about human beings as a whole?

Education

One formative event in a child's life is their education. Good teaching can shape a child's personality, in a socio-economic and nurturing way. It can be a road to freedom. Those smart enough can use the education system to make their way into a well-paid profession. In turn, this should reward their children who will be born into a comfortable socio-economic life.

Although is only true in our modern-day industrialized times. Though, it doesn't guarantee that children from a stable economic background will be happy and well balanced. It only serves to increase their life chances. Whether they take advantage of that will depend on how their personality develops. Even children from wealthy backgrounds can be abused and scarred. It's not only socio-economics that influence our lives, but also the comfort of love and stability.

A child's personality is only partly dependent on the genes they inherit. Other influencing factors are parents, teachers, and even peer groups. Though without education, a child cannot grow to fit into the socio-economic developments they live within. Education can provide us with opportunities, even those from a poor background. Although, it will be more difficult for them to be successful, but not impossible.

Much of what is on offer MUST flow with stability for the child to develop into a well-balanced adult. Should anything tip that balance, such as a traumatic life event, the positive side of personality development will be at risk. There's a lot at play, and it only takes someone with a dark personality to come along and tip that balance. A child with a stable background can take advantage of a good education, and that's no matter what their socio-economical status is. It is the interconnection of nature and nurture that plays an important part in our developing personalities.

You cannot take either nature or nurture out of the equation, they both play equal roles in our personality development.

It's almost like an equation:

- ➢ Behavior and attitude of carers.
- ➢ Plus availability of a good education.

> Plus inherited genes.

> All equal personality.

This shows that a person's personality is a pot of many features, all helping to shape each of us as individuals.

Chapter 8

CAN PEOPLE CHANGE THEIR PERSONALITY?

We have shown that a person's personality can be fluid with age, as we live through our life experiences.

Is it possible to change the parts of our personality that we don't like?

Can we evolve into becoming a better person during our lifetime?

The good news is that scientific says, "yes," we can alter certain behaviors that we're unhappy with.

The not so good news is that it is hard work and cognitively taxing. You cannot wake up one morning and tell yourself not to be a grouch with everyone at work. Within an hour of being there, your subconscious will kick in and you'll be back to your old self. And, there lays the biggest problem! To change your personality, you need to control the subconscious, and that's no easy task. It's taken all your years of life to become the person you are. You don't have another life to live, so you will need to work hard, and fast, to change this one. Plus, there's also the problem of those inherited genes.

Can you alter the biological parts of your body, such as hormones and genes?

Around 40-50% of your genes are inherited. But, numerous observational studies have indicated that you can also change those parts of your personality. It's not about the genetic coding but more about how your conscious mind works.

Let's look at a couple of ways that might help you change your personality.

Clinical Intervention

> ➢ Therapy or counselling is one solution. This could mean one-to-one, or it could take the form of group therapy, such as anger or addiction management.

Studies are showing that it's easier to treat certain traits, such as anxiety and depression. Whereas treating illnesses such as addiction or personality disorders are much more difficult. Beginning therapeutic sessions as soon as possible might help to stop anxiety setting in for too long. That in itself could prevent you from becoming an addict. Prolonged depression that goes untreated, can have a devastating effect on your personality

Another problem is that it's not a simple task to measure the results of therapy. Therapists are more focussed on treating specific problems rather than the personality as a whole. They don't set out to alter a person's personality. They tend to help in easing mental health conditions, such as anxiety or depression. Could this even be considered as changing your personality? If you don't suffer from mental health issues, you may not be able to get professional help. There is also the issue, in certain countries, that health insurance doesn't cover therapy, and it may be too expensive a solution.

The biggest influencing factor is the patient themselves. Success relies on how much they WANT to change. Studies show that for someone determined enough, they can expect good results as early as the first month. Progress tends to plateaux at around three months. Even when therapy stops the positives continue. It looks like professional therapy can work. Like everything else in life, we do better at being successful if we have direction and encouragement.

Changing Your personality all by Yourself

We all live in an ever-changing world. Humans play a huge part in those changes. Make sure that you're on the right side of those changes and not only taking but also giving. Play a positive role so that when another person analyzes you, they will see a good person.

- ➢ It is possible to achieve this, but the participant MUST be self-motivated.
- ➢ That's because it's all about changing your habits.

Habits take years to shape, and you're about to unshape them. You will need to retrain yourself in your daily practices. Do you think you can force changes and in your thinking patterns? Whatever your answer, you owe it to yourself to give it a go.

Do want others to see you as a well-balanced person when they're analyzing you?

If not, then you need to understand what good personality qualities are.

There are few of us who are calm and patient souls by nature. For those who dare to admit that they aren't, get ready to learn how to become such a person.

If you're happy being an anxious or aggressive person, then it's unlikely you can ever change. It seems that you feel comfortable with who you are. Or, are you living in denial? Those who can't admit their faults are blinded by their own deceit. Because they don't see their faults, they will never seek to better themselves

For the rest of you, well done, you've admitted to your faults and want to become a better person. A person who others will perceive as reliable and well balanced.

How do you change your personality?

Identify your faults, and admit to them.

This can be much harder than you might think because most of us are in denial. Look deep inside your conscience and search for the smaller details of your behavior. Ask yourself questions that will cause you to confront your darker behavior, such as

Do you take your anxiety out on others?

Do you become an angry person when you drive?

Does noise annoy you?

You're looking for all that dark behavior that's hidden away. One way to do this task is to write a journal for a week. Another way is to speak into a recorder, such as your phone, about your feelings as they happen. You will need to write, or speak, about your emotions as often as you can.

What makes you feel happy, at peace, angry, annoyed?

You might be surprised by your discoveries, and there are going to be lots of them.

For instance:

- ➢ You may come to realize that you hate driving in the rush hour.

- ➢ Or, the noise of children playing either annoys you, or makes you feel happy.

Listen out to the noises around you, such as bird cheeping, traffic, airplanes passing over. We are so good at cutting out peripheral sounds that we almost become deaf and blind to what's going on around us. To understand yourself, you need to start focusing on the periphery around you, as you move about your day.

Let's create a **case scenario** for a fictional person:

- ➢ John gets up before his wife and children because he has to get to work early.

- He's in the bathroom with the lights on because it's still dark outside, rushing into the shower and out again.
- There's no time to eat breakfast because he has to drive through the rush hour traffic.
- Arriving at work, he always gets a semi-cold coffee from the vending machine because the coffee shop has a long queue.
- Switching on his computer, he taps away at the keyboard to read all the emails that he hasn't had a chance to reply to. There are way too many!
- As his assistant comes into his office, he yells at her because he wishes she was more competent in organizing his workload. He senses she doesn't like him much but he doesn't care. Instead, he instructs her to go and get him a sandwich, something he does every day. It frustrates him that she will now disappear for an age, to join the long line waiting in the coffee shop.
- Finally, at around eleven, he gets to eat the sandwich his assistant has brought to him. Plus, she made him a fresh coffee that he drinks but never notices.

- In half an hour he has a two-hour-long meeting to attend, so he needs to eat fast. At least there will be pastries at the meeting so he can grab a bite there. Except he has to do a presentation and may not have time to eat, so he could end up hungry and thirsty after the meeting.

- After the meeting, he is indeed dehydrated and it gives him a headache. Needless to say, this puts him in a worse mood than he was already in. It will last for the rest of the afternoon. It doesn't help that he suffers constipation because he doesn't eat properly. It annoys him that keeps needing to go to the bathroom. Nor does he wants anyone to notice, so he tends to ignore everyone he passes if he's on a trip to the bathroom. His colleagues expect him to ignore them, so they don't bother him much. He's known as the office grouch.

- Traffic home is much the same as it was going to work, honking horns, rude finger remarks, and much grinding of teeth.

- When he arrives home he's grouchy to his wife and children too. Finally, he gets a good meal, which he chooses to eat on his own while watching his favorite sport on the TV. He doesn't notice that his wife and children are laughing and enjoying their meal together at the dining room table. He's switched off from peripheral sounds and is only focusing on the TV.

- After his meal, he goes to his study to work, those emails still need answering and there's such a long, long list of them.

- By the time he goes to bed, his wife is fast asleep, snoring lightly. That annoys him because he can't sleep. He goes into the spare room, considering getting a separate bed from his wife. It's not as if they have much sex these days, she's too busy snoring.

- Before he knows it, his alarm goes off and he's off to the shower again.

John is an ordinary guy living his life. Every one of us is living out our own special story. Each life is unique and each life is important.

John is successful in providing for his family, but he's not a happy or content person. In fact, he rarely smiles. Even when they take a vacation together he finds it hard work. There's always stuff to organize so his family doesn't moan at him. Does this guy ever enjoy life?

There are ways to change this vicious cycle. First, though, he needs to recognize and admit that much of what is wrong in his life is down to him. If he's willing to do that, then there are ways to help him enjoy the life he's living.

Exercise 1 Breathing Relaxation

The moment you wake up, don't rush out of bed. Instead, lay on your back and learn how to do breathing relaxation.

Start by taking in a deep breath, through your nose or mouth, whichever is most comfortable. Allow your stomach to expand like a balloon to take in lots of oxygen.

Hold it for a couple of seconds.

Let it out, through your nose or mouth, again, whichever is most comfortable.

Repeat at least 3-4 times or as many times as you need to help you feel calm.

Exercise 2 Focus on the Now

As you take a shower, think about the experience of the water on your skin. Feel the warmth, or coolness, of the water as it beats against your body. Allow it to trickle down your face, eyes closed of course, and ask yourself what you feel. Spend no more time in the shower than you need, but focus on the entire experience as you're in there. Smell the scent of the soap, feel the sensation of the sponge if you use one.

By focusing your mind on this one task, you're not worrying about anything else. For a short while, your mind is calm. You'll feel much better afterward for those quality moments in your day. Try and do this exercise with other tasks in your day, such as when you eat food. Smell the food, chew slower so you can enjoy the flavors. Think about the ingredients and simply enjoy the sensation of eating.

It's all about focus. Your mind can't think about more than one thing at a time. Instead of running all your worries through your mind as you eat, focus on the task at hand. Allow all the other worries of the world to take a back seat for a few short moments.

Exercise 3 Avoid Anxiety

Play soothing music in the car, whatever it is that relaxes YOU, as we all like different tunes. As you're stuck in traffic, look around you, but maintain your concentration on the traffic too. If you're surrounded by concrete buildings, connect with nature for a few moments by looking at a tree. Admire the architect of historical buildings. If you pass a recreational park, imagine you're walking through it as you drive by. All visual image that will help your mind relax.

Sure, you do need to be concentrating on the traffic, but your mind can be telling you a little story as you plow through the city roads. That way you won't be honking your horn because the car in front of you took a second too long to pull off.

If your journey is so monotonous and boring that it's become a dreaded chore, break it up into a few zones in your mind. Where will you put the mid-point zone? Because after that you're on countdown, you're almost at your destination. You're telling your mind that after that point, you can be positive, the trip is almost over. Mind over matter can have a strong influence over your well-being.

If you've done it right, your entire journey has been spent with your mind thinking positive thoughts. All the while the soothing music played in the background. Much better than having head-banging sounds pounding in your head.

Okay, parking can be a nightmare when you arrive at work. And so the stress levels begin to rocket. Even worse, you spotted a space and some moron beat you to it. STOP! THINK! Don't give them the finger or shout at them. Stay calm! Stress raises your heart rate and blood pressure, which is problematic in itself. Imagine yourself swimming in a warm ocean as soon as you're ready to explode. Think positive thoughts as you search for another spot. Create a way, in your mind, of dealing with such situations as they arise, because it's inevitable that they will. So, the other guy got in first, so what? Is that a threat to your life? NO! It is not. Well, actually, it is if you allow your stress levels to take over

When you arrive in the office, go out of your way to smile casually at someone. That smile will make you feel better inside, and it will have a positive effect on the other person too. Do anything that stops you from feeling annoyed. Force positive thoughts into your head, your heart will thank you for it.

It's going to take time to learn to think like this. If you fail a few times, don't punish yourself. Keep trying, keep trying, keep trying.

Eventually, you'll arrive at work feeling happier with yourself. After all, you gave up your parking spot for someone else. You made other people feel positive with your friendly smiles. You spotted things on your journey that you've never even noticed before. Observe the world around you instead of focusing on getting to work and all the tasks you have to do when you get there. Those tasks are not going anywhere and they'll still be there when you arrive. Forget about them for a short while and allow other, more positive thoughts to come into your head.

Solutions for John

John can't change his daily routine, but he can look outside the box to see that there's a world around him, such as:

- Why not join the line in the coffee shop? Speak to other people while you're in there and enjoy the small talk for a few moments of the day. At the end of it, he'll get a better coffee than the vending machine rubbish.

- Ask his assistant to purchase two lunches so they can eat together as they discuss his workload. Organize the files on his computer so he can deal with the urgent messages first. Moving the non-urgent ones into a specific file to be dealt with later. Set aside a certain time in the week to tackle them so they don't get overlooked. It doesn't need to be a perfect solution but if it eases the task only a little, it's worth implementing.

- He's better off not eating the pastries in the meeting anyway. He should get into the habit of taking a bottle of water with him into every meeting. He can take small sips as he does his presentation. Dehydration can lead to many medical issues. No doubt it's the cause of his headaches and constipation.

- Why, oh why, isn't he eating dinner with his family? It's the best opportunity of the day to listen to his children and ask them what happened in their day. How about thanking his wife for such a lovely meal. What a great way of communicating with his family, over dinner. All too soon they'll be grown up and won't have time for him anymore. Instill the habit that family dinners are important so you can all talk to each other.

- The other obvious habit he needs to break is that he should be going out of his way to communicate with his wife better. No doubt she's had a busy day too. After all, she also contributes to the home, either by working to help the family finances, or as a housewife. Look out for all the little things that other people do for you, and thank them for it at some point.

This was an exercise to show you how easy it can be for ordinary people to add a little quality time into their daily lives. Breathing techniques can be used at any time of the day, even seated or standing. It helps to take your mind away from an anxious moment and allow you to calm down. Particularly so if you can learn to visualize happy images.

Anxiety can be the cause of so many negative parts of our personality, but it doesn't need to be that way. All you have to do is take control and focus on the good things in life. They are there, but you've lost your way. Visualize images that make you feel content and use them when you're under stress.

How to Control Anxiety

Anxiety is a response that your body uses to protect you. It's part of the mechanism known as "fight, flight, or freeze." In the hunter-gatherer days, it could have saved your life. Such reactions lead to your body creating specific chemicals from your glands. This sends messages to your brain, to force a few moments of extra strength and alertness. It's exactly what you need should you be in danger. Or, in any situation where you need an extra boost of adrenalin, such as an interview or public speaking. The specific chemicals will assist your body to get you through the unusual situation. It's when that alertness lasts for too long that it can lead to your body overworking. This is prolonged anxiety, which leads to anxiety disorders.

No matter your type of personality, our bodies all work in much the same way. Some of us know how to control anxiety and calm ourselves down. Others do not, and they're the ones at risk of mental illness. It shows how our bodies are ruled by hormonal chemicals, but you can learn to control the release of them. You CAN take charge of your body.

The chemical produced during stress is known as Cortisol, which is a steroid hormone. If you learn to recognize when you are feeling anxious, you can deal with it immediately. Even something as simple as doing a short burst of relaxation breathing exercises will help. It works in a similar way as counting to ten before you shout. It helps you pull away from the situation that's causing you stress, while you concentrate your mind on another task. There is also medication that helps with hormonal imbalances, but you must see a professional to be prescribed the right amount.

Here are a few tips that can help you keep stress at bay:

Getting Organized

Having a good routine in your life helps you to be more efficient and ensure everything gets done. There's nothing worse than feeling out of control. Simple things, such as eating three meals a day, or doing certain important tasks on set days. To achieve some organization in your life, get into the habit of creating lists. That way you can see what tasks need to be completed and give them all time constraints. Build up the list until you've included EVERYTHING that will help to give you peace of mind. It may take months to achieve, but as you build it up, you'll find that you're getting better organized.

Doing Quality Exercise

On that list don't forget to include some exercise in your daily routine. Whether it means walking to work on a Wednesday, or going swimming on a Friday, make sure it's on that TO-DO list. Exercise doesn't help you lose weight unless you do a lot of it, but it will keep your heart and mind healthier. Particularly if you can include a few nature walks in parks or woodlands. Trees and water settings make very relaxing healthy walks.

Getting Quality Rest

This is much more important to us than most of us realize. Without a doubt, if you're sleep deprived you're going to feel agitated and anxious. If you have trouble sleeping, learn to lay in your bed at night where you are relaxing at the very least. Ditch that caffeine after lunchtime. Try not to eat after six, or seven, at night. Use breathing exercises to help you relax. Those chemicals in your body are not behaving as they should, and you must do what it takes to slow them down.

Writing a Journal

Another task that has shown to be useful for peace of mind, is to journal your day. Write all that stuff that's rattling around in your head, onto a piece of paper, or computer. Jotting down your emotions is a great way to unburden yourself. Tell yourself who and what situations annoyed you today. Have a good old moan to yourself! Tear the paper up afterward if you're worried someone will read it. The important part is the "talking to yourself" about your troubles. That voice in your head can be a great friend. There's no harm in telling yourself all your woes because at least you know that you'll listen to yourself. By writing it all down you're getting off your chest. Go for it!

Healthy Eating

Try and eat home-made cooking as much as you can. That tomato sauce in a jar will almost certainly have added sugar and excessive salt. Instead, grab a tin of chopped tomatoes, add your own herbs and salt, keeping then sauce much healthier. This is only one example, but you can never be sure what rubbish that manufactured food has in it. Home cooking is much healthier and tastier because you are in control.

Also, make sure you drink plenty every day. We've shown that dehydration can lead to health issues so make sure you drink, and not alcohol or caffeine, they don't count. Talking of alcohol, don't participate in drinking too much of it. You know it's not good for you, so be careful.

Stop Smoking

JUST STOP! That's it. It's expensive, it makes you stink, and it's likely to kill you sooner rather than later. Try vaping instead, if you're struggling to cut it out. Try anything - but you must stop.

Those are but a few tips to help you have a healthier body. If you have more days feeling healthier, this will have an impact on your wellbeing. The more content you feel, the happier your emotions. Also, the stronger you are to cope with negative events as they come at you.

It's not only about your personality, but also about keeping a healthy mind and body.

Discontentment of the self

There are many people, besides yourself, who would love to alter certain things about themselves. Things that make them feel and look bad when other people are assessing and analyzing them.

One study, in 2014, came up with some interesting analysis:

- ➢ Those unhappy with their friendships wished they could be more extrovert.
- ➢ Those dissatisfied with their financial status and general achievements in life wished they could learn how to be more conscientious. Although 97% of candidates fell into this bracket.

As we age we tend to become more discontent with the shortcomings in our lives. This can cause a shift in our values as we attempt to improve ourselves. That's why Americans as a whole spend billions of dollars on self-improvement. They may:

- ➢ Attend seminars to learn how to become more confident.
- ➢ Buy books on how to be more successful.
- ➢ Pay for a life-coach.
- ➢ Join a self-improvement group.

It seems that some of us are committed to investing a lot of effort and time into our personal growth.

It's important though not to set too many goals, or set them too high, or you may fall at the first post.

Let's do a case scenario:

For the sake of our scenario, let's assume that you are a shy person. You often find other's distancing themselves from you and it upsets you. This makes you want to become more of an extravert. At least then others would notice you, because at the moment you feel like other people don't even know you exist.

The biggest obstacle is that you can't learn to become extrovert overnight. Ask yourself, is that even what is needed? Sure, extrovert personalities are noticed more. But, if you're not already a loud outgoing person then the chances are that you never will be. Instead of setting your goals at being more extrovert, why not reach out to be more noticeable in a different way? What you need to do is to show others that you have got skills. It could be that you're a genuine empathic person who likes to help others. Or, you're clever with maths or good at a particular sport. Find something that you're good at and feel confident enough to share, and look at pushing that skill forward. Of course, others don't know about your skills because you're too shy to talk to them. Don't worry, we're getting to that next.

You need to learn how to become more talkative, and not how to become more extravert. By talking more, it should help you to tackle that shyness too. It won't change your personality overnight, but it will help you to come out of your shell. One of the heavier burdens of being shy is that you worry others think you talk nonsense. Perhaps you do, but it could also be in your imagination.

Set out a plan of action. First, only include people who you feel confident with already. When you feel you've hit the first stage, go on to the next stage in your plan. This needs to be easy, such as including talking to one person a day who you don't know very well. Even if it's only to say good morning.

Your plan of action should not be too hard to achieve, so you don't end up feeling that you've failed. Avoid a cycle of constant disappointments by not setting your goals too high. For example, consider someone who's trying to lose weight. If that weight doesn't go down every day, or week, then they tend to feel they've failed. They'll try again, and fail again. it's a vicious circle that may lead to them giving up altogether. Accept that you are going to struggle and have disappointing days. Aim for smaller goals ie talk to one stranger a week instead of every day, if that's more likely to work for you. Every time you achieve your goal, record it. That way, you can see on a chart that you're gaining ground with your confidence.

Make those targets small and realistic. When you achieve it, make another small target. Every part of your plan must be done in baby steps. You can't rush to change those habits that you've taken your whole life to build up. The new you is going to feel alien because you'll be forcing new ways of behaving upon your established old self.

CONCLUSION

Did you ever think there would be so much involved in learning to understand the people around you?

Only if you first analyze yourself can you qualify to assess other people with an open and honest evaluation. To analyze other people, you must ensure that your baseline beliefs are fair. If they're not, then you risk prejudicing your results.

This book could not cover every aspect of the complexities of human behavior. There are far too many! What it can do is open the door to your understanding. Your own curiosity should then lead you to deeper research. That's the only way to increase your knowledge of the workings of the human mind.

Even the sciences cannot yet comprehend the full intricacies of the human brain. Throughout your analysis, you can only touch upon the surface of why people behave as they do. Unless you know every detail of an individual's life's experiences, all you can do is assess them with an open mind. For example, let's say you're confronted by someone with road rage. It would be foolish to try and calm them as you are their target. If you have an understanding of why a person may be so aggressive you'll know to remain calm and quiet. The person before you may not be a bad person. They may have experienced traumatic problems that are incomprehensible to most of us. You can't tackle that, but you can empathize with them. Don't blame them because they have social issues. Though, if you're in any danger, make sure there is a distance between you both. You must never confront a person with dark traits ruling their personality. Such people must be treated with caution. But, you'll know this, because you've researched and read books on it.

Unless you're a professional psychologist, then analyzing other people is a difficult process. By reading this book, you will at least learn where to begin. Analyzing people takes time to learn. Let's say you want to assess why someone's aggressive, then you must factor in their life experiences. Most particularly whether they had a traumatic childhood. And even more so, if they have received little, or no, love and support as a child.

Some people will never change their personality because they don't see themselves as having any faults.

Such people have a right to stay as they are, but what will they achieve in their lives? Will they ever be successful in their careers and personal lives? Will they ever be popular? It's most likely that they'll always be at the back of the line of people who are truly content with their lives.

It's also important to reassess yourself first. Make sure you have an open mind if you're going to be judging other people's behavior. A closed mind will be influenced by their own beliefs. That will not give you the broad conclusion that you need when observing other people's behavior.

It's one thing to become popular because we can all fake the words that come out of our mouths to make other's believe we're leaders. Politicians do it all the time. They lie and bribe their way into popularity, but can they stay there? Yes, it's another thing to keep that popularity going. Others will judge you by your true behavior. Politicians are well known for not backing their promises. A deceitful person can only manipulate others for so long. There will be so many behavioral signals that eventually give them away, if you know what to look for.

This book has opened up the way to understanding why people behave as they do. It includes the darker personality traits that show ways of spotting a manipulator or a liar. It also shows you how to assess your own personality. Only then can you legitimately go on to analyze other people with a fair and truthful process.

www.ingramcontent.com/pod-product-compliance
Lightning Source LLC
Chambersburg PA
CBHW020257030426
42336CB00010B/809